JUST ONE MORE SMILE

Fred & Helen Archer's
Tragic Love Story

By

Diana Reynolds

This book is sold subject to the condition that it shall not, by way of trade or otherwise, be lent, resold, hired out, or otherwise circulated without the publisher's prior consent in any form of binding or cover other than that in which it is published and without a similar condition including this condition being imposed on the subsequent publisher.
The moral right of Diana Reynolds has been asserted.
ISBN-13: 978-1537385006
ISBN-10: 1537385003

To Mum, whom I still miss every day, and to all my grandchildren, pure joy.

CONTENTS

PROLOGUE 1
CHAPTER ONE 4
CHAPTER TWO 24
CHAPTER THREE 46
CHAPTER FOUR 70
CHAPTER FIVE 87
CHAPTER SIX... 103
CHAPTER SEVEN 130
CHAPTER EIGHT 154
CHAPTER NINE 173
CHAPTER TEN 195
CHAPTER ELEVEN 213
CHAPTER TWELVE 229
AFTERWORD 250
ABOUT THE AUTHOR 256

This is a work of creative biographical fiction. This book has not been created to be specific to any individual's or organizations' situation or needs. Every effort has been made to make this book as accurate as possible. This book should serve only as a general guide and not as the ultimate source of subject information. The author shall have no liability or responsibility to any person or entity regarding any loss or damage incurred, or alleged to have incurred, directly or indirectly, by the information contained in this book.

PROLOGUE

Fred opened his eyes slowly. His body ached, he felt dizzy and tremendously thirsty. He also had the strangest feeling like he was there, but not really there.

He turned over lazily, expecting to see his beloved Helen, but he was alone. The bed was a crumpled mass of white sheets, with unruly peaks and troughs, but there was no one hidden within its folds. Fred struggled to focus. It couldn't be right. Helen was meant to be there. She was always meant to be by his side. They had made promises to one another. They would be together forever. That is what they had said.

Then, to his relief, he caught sight of the door beyond the bed slowly opening. He caught his breath. Could it be? Could it? Yes, it was her. His lovely wife was standing there, in a beautiful, white, lace-covered dress that flowed down her perfect figure, accentuating every curve. She was smiling at him and looked like she was about to say something. Oh, how he always loved that knowing pout of hers. One hand was on her hip and their son, William Junior, clutched

Helen's other hand tightly. He had the unsteadiness of all toddlers, but looked proud to be standing on his own two feet. He was smartly dressed in a crisp blue and white sailor's outfit.

Fred smiled. It was a long, languid smile of pleasure. These people were his life. All that he needed. His everything. Helen looked between Fred and William Junior and laughed softly.

Then, to Fred's horror, the image began to fade. It was as though someone had slowly began to shade over the pair at the door using a white pencil in even strokes, starting from their feet. Bit by torturous bit their forms began to gradually vanish into the background.

Fred sat up. He was panicking now. He couldn't lose them. He wanted them back. He needed them. Life would be meaningless without them. All this would be for nothing. The house, the fame, the money. Everything.

He gasped for breath because he could barely see them now. Only the dark irises of Helen's eyes and the barest outline of her rosebud lips could be seen. The short dark curls of William Junior's hair were all that were left to show of his son.

Fred pawed at his bedside drawer. A protective animal instinct had taken over. He needed his revolver. He was prepared to fight and give everything for what was his.

He shouted out: 'Are they coming...'

The word 'back' died on his lips as he saw they had vanished altogether now. Feeling a rising tide of despair he leapt to his feet. He was shocked to find some hidden force was grabbing at his wrist, stopping him from going to his family. He struggled against this interloper with all his strength. He had to save Helen and William Junior. He had to get them back. He didn't care what happened to him. He only had one thought on his mind.

Somehow, he didn't know how, he pushed the unseen foe back and staggered to the door. Staring wildly about himself he searched for his wife and son. He could not see through a black mist that was slowly masking his eyes though. It was enveloping him and choking him. He was drowning. Was he about to disappear too? All he knew now was he mustn't let it, them, whatever it was, get him. He lifted the weapon. He had to protect Helen and William Junior. He had to do the right thing. His finger found the trigger. His heart found the strength.

A shot rang out.

CHAPTER ONE

The significance of the timing of the announcement went unnoticed to all but Emma. Her son, Fred, at just eleven years old, had been invited to become an apprentice to Mat Dawson, the renowned Newmarket trainer. It was the exact same age that her husband, Fred's father, William, had run away from his parents to seek fame and fortune on the racecourse. The difference was, William Archer was tough. He always had been. His appearance today bore witness to this. He was a rough man in appearance and habits, short, stocky and pugnacious, with a mouth permanently filled with language bad enough to make a navvy blush. Fred, on the other hand, was sensitive, shy, nervous and quiet.

Fred had undoubtedly inherited his temperament and indeed looks from his mother. Emma, the daughter of a Cheltenham innkeeper and the niece of a respected clergyman, was soft voiced and sweet-natured, almost aristocratic in looks, elegance, and poise. Her perfect pale skin perfectly set off her dark brown eyes and her neatly tied-back, glossy chestnut hair always neatly framed her pretty face. Fred, although painfully thin and still adolescent, had similar looks, except he had a mop of unruly black hair. It was his deep brown eyes that were most striking though. They were almost bewitching.

Fred was a bright boy, but despite Emma's protestations, he was barely allowed to study. He was plonked onto a horse almost as soon as he could walk.

'Come on Fred,' William would bark, as Emma wrung her hands in concern. 'Lift your legs up in those bloody stirrups and tuck your head down. You'll never get the rhythm if you don't do as I bloody showed you!'

His future was, it seemed, all mapped out. William Archer had achieved his ambition, winning the Grand National in 1858 on Little Charlie and he was damn well going to make sure he continued his legacy. William and Emma had five children, Alice, Emily, William, Frederick, and Charles. Although all three Archer boys rode, Fred who had been born just a year before the big win, was, without a doubt, the anointed successor.

'I know he has a good seat and could make something of himself,' William would say to anyone who would listen, most usually the assembled throng in the Kings Arms. The Kings Arms was the pub left to the Archers by Emma's father Bill Hayward and brought them a meagre income over and above what William earned with horses. The other regulars would nod in agreement and pass their tankards up the bar to be topped up by the landlord. They'd heard it all before, but knew that when William was on his soapbox about Fred they could wheedle a drink or two from him for free.

Emma wasn't sure though. She rather fancied that a sensitive soul like her son would be better suited to the cloth. She could see him as a parson and urged William to let him study more often.

'If he's got an education behind him, he'll do so much better for himself,' she'd say to her husband quietly as they sat in the parlour, after the children had retired to bed.

'Let the lad alone; he'll make more out of his riding than he ever will out of book-learning,' William retorted with an angry and dismissive swipe of his hand.

Emma would look at her husband, her eyes full of sadness and her heart heavy. More than once she asked herself why she ever married this brash man. William, had come from a family of thirteen children, and had always been attractive to the ladies, not least because of his colourful past. He had spent time in Russia, at the personal request of the Tsar who wanted him to look after his horses. However, he also had a temper on him and did not seem to know how to sugar his words if he wanted his own way. Emma did love him, but things could have been so different, if, if… The alternative image was a frequent visitor to her mind, but she always pushed it, him, away. This was her bed. She must lie in it. William Archer was a good man and a father to her lovely children.

That didn't mean Emma was ready to give up on all her dreams though.

'I do wish you would let me school them more,' she'd press, when she felt William was in a good mood. 'I know racing is in your blood, but Fred is an intelligent boy. I would hope that he could be taught there is pleasure to be had in books and writing too.'

Each time though, she was rebuffed.

'The lad is fine,' William would growl, his good mood evaporating the moment the subject came up. 'He has a way with a pony and there is no fear in him. I have not seen it before in such a youngster, so let him be. Spend your teaching hours on the girls, I will not protest on that, my dear.'

Emma would always back down wearily. She couldn't escape the notion that the only reason Fred rode at all was to please his father. She certainly couldn't imagine how he could derive any pleasure from being shouted at so much about his technique.

Emma's nervousness about Fred's destiny was made worse the first time he fell off a horse, aged just five years old. William had won a Galloway pony, called Chard, in a raffle and poor Fred was made to almost constantly practise his riding in the courtyard of the Kings Arms, come rain or shine. Emma could hardly bear to watch the tiny form gamely trotting around the yard, going over and over small hurdles, holding on for dear life while William shouted and cursed until he was satisfied with Fred's seat.

Emma had been inside the inn, clearing away bottles with the help of her daughter Emily when she heard a commotion. With a sixth sense she knew it was her son and they both dashed through the dimly lit corridor towards the back door.

The sight that greeted Emma made her gasp. Her son's small, delicate form was lying in a twisted heap on the wet cobbles, the rain still lashing down around him, one leg in the air, with a foot firmly wedged in the stirrup. What upset her most was the look on Fred's face. Although he had clearly hurt himself, the overwhelming emotion his look conveyed was anger and disappointment with himself. Her husband's campaign was clearly bearing fruit. Her son was furious with himself for failing.

'It's all right Father, my foot slipped out of the stirrup,' Fred said, struggling to free his trapped other foot. 'It was my fault. I was not pushing down hard enough.'

Neither of them had even noticed Emma standing at the door, one hand clasped over her mouth in concern, while the other gripped a large handful of her white apron so hard her knuckles were white. She was similarly oblivious to the steadily falling rain that soaked through her flimsy blouse.

William had chuckled silently to himself, shaking his head, as he made his way over to Fred. Without ceremony, he lifted him up by his collar, deftly twisting him around so he sat back on Chard. His trapped foot never left the stirrup.

Emma had seen enough.

'What are you doing William?' she shouted. The pair turned around in shock. It was rare for Emma to raise her voice. 'Leave him alone. It's freezing out here. He's only little, give it a rest before he…'

Her voice faltered and abruptly broke off. William was glaring at her. She'd gone too far.

Fred looked at his father and then his mother. Even at his tender age, he sensed a tremendous tussle of wills. The trouble was, they both wanted such different things of him.

'I'm all right Mama, don't fuss,' Fred broke in, giving a reassuring smile to his mother as he straightened up in his saddle. 'This yard is not big enough, so Chard slipped on the cobbles.'

Leaning forward he slapped his mount on its neck playfully.

'Come on Chard, I will ride you once more round the yard so you know I'm not frightened. Then I will come in.'

William nodded with approval and Emma turned to go back inside with a tut, grabbing her daughter's hand as she swept past. This was not a battle she would win anytime soon. It broke her heart to see her precious son being pushed so hard. William's training regime was draconian to say the least.

If the incident in the courtyard was bad enough, there was worse to follow. Shortly after Fred's eighth birthday, William put him up for his first race.

The match, which would see Fred and Chard pitched against a local lad called Pete on his donkey, was twice around the orchard of the Plough Inn, with a brook to be jumped each time. Emma didn't want her son to ride, but knew well enough by now she'd have little say in the matter. To calm herself down, she hand-tailored a magnificent set of silk colours for him to wear, sewing her love and protection into each stitch.

On the day of the race itself, Fred looked so grown-up and proud in his new outfit, Emma checked herself for not supporting him enough. She'd just wanted him to be happy and safe though.

'Good luck,' she whispered, giving his shoulder a squeeze. She wanted to add: 'and please be careful,' but she knew he'd hate that.

'Luck has nothing to do with it, it is all about training,' Fred said, his face solemn and apprehensive.

These weren't his words. Emma knew that. They were straight out of William's stock-in-trade of boastful phrases.

There was no time to think about that now though. Fred on Chard and Pete on his donkey were ready for the off. Emma noticed with a start that Pete was brandishing a thick stick. It looked like a long piece of willow that had carefully been whittled down.

There was barely time to think about it before the starter signalled the beginning of the race and the two were off. Pete immediately brought his stick into play, bringing it sharply down on his ride's rump, delivering a stinging blow. The poor donkey almost shrieked in fright and surprise and bolted forward at a tremendous rate, its eyes wide and nostrils flared. The line of people who had turned out to watch on the hot sunny day cheered in approval. Fred was already far behind, urging poor Chard on by digging his heels in, his chin jutting forward in determination. Nothing he did was enough though. With Pete's stick flashing up and down in the sunlight, his donkey romped home, well ahead of Fred.

Poor Fred. Emma could see he was utterly shattered and broken up inside by the defeat. His shoulders slumped and he slipped off Chard with barely a backwards glance, leaving William to grab at the reins. Emma watched, her eyes welling with tears of concern, as Fred walked past the crowds, without ever once looking up. He carried on walking, all the way home, without saying a word to anyone. Once there, he ran to his room, threw himself onto his bed and cried deep, rasping sobs of shame. He had lost his first race.

If Emma had hoped this race would put an end to William's ambitions, she was to be sorely disappointed. Worse still, it wasn't just William who saw the defeat as a 'minor setback' on the road to glory, it was Fred too. Indeed, her son's grief rapidly turned into anger. He cast around, going over and over the race in his head, to work out why he had lost. His conclusion, the only conclusion he could come to, was he had not been tough enough.

'If you want to win, you have to try every trick in the book,' he said, more to himself than anyone in particular.

Barely three hours after the end of the race, Fred was heading to the river bank to get himself a willow stick.

Three weeks later, a rematch was set. This time Fred borrowed a donkey called Charlie from a friend. He didn't want to jinx his chances by returning with Chard. Still stinging from defeat, he and William planned their strategy meticulously.

'Right son, this time let Pete think he has the better of you until you reach the far end,' William said, speaking urgently, banging one fist into his palm for emphasis. 'He will then ease up and that's when to strike. Raise yourself high up in the saddle and give Charlie a good kick. That will wake him up and then you go. By the time Pete sees what's going on you'll be in the home stretch. Good luck and let's see your first win!'

Emma listened in silence. The thought flashed through her mind that perhaps it would be better if Fred lost. Then maybe this whole silly dream of another Grand National champion in the family would die a natural death and Fred would be allowed to get on with a career better suited to his temperament. But, she knew William would never let it drop. He'd keep goading and goading their son till he fulfilled his dream. She just wished Fred had a chance to dream his own dreams. It never seemed fair to her that one's life dreams could so easily be crushed and forgotten.

Fred jumped on Charlie's back and urged his donkey forward to line up with Pete. This time, only a dozen or so locals had come out to watch, since the weather was slightly inclement. Even so, the atmosphere in the orchard was tense. William had made such a big deal about the re-match, everyone felt sure they were in for a treat. Yet, could Fred deliver?

The flag went down and off they went. Pete did just as he had done a few weeks before and his donkey raced off in a desperate and doomed bid to escape the cruel beating. Fred followed at a good pace and, just as he came to the last apple tree at the bottom of the orchard, gave his donkey a whack with his own willow whip, while simultaneously digging his heels sharply into its sides. He hung on grimly as Charlie seemed to leap into the air, his ears pinned back, before surging forward. In an instant, Fred was close to catching up with Pete.

When Fred sped by, his bottom in the air, Pete was so surprised he nearly dropped his reins. His face was a picture. The small gathering roared at the sight of Fred, three years Pete's junior, taking the win. Fred raised his hand in triumph as Charlie went past the two empty barrels that formed the winning posts. His face betrayed the pure joy he felt at winning his first race and he beamed at his father and mother.

From that moment on, Fred's fate was sealed. There was no stopping William now and Fred was, without a doubt, a willing participant in the race to be the next winner in the family. Although he trained alongside his brothers, William Junior and Charles, the focus was definitely on Fred. After stepping up Fred's training schedule, William did a deal with Charles Pullen, the landlord of the Unicorn at Winchcombe, paying £5 for a 12.2 hand-high pony called Moss Rose. Fred adored Moss Rose from the start and willingly practised on her day and night. He'd even mumble her name in his sleep. Moss Rose, for her part, seemed to feel the same way. From being a pony that threw most of those impertinent enough to try climbing on her back, she meekly allowed Fred to ride her four or five hours a day. The pair seemed to have a mutual understanding.

Aged ten, Fred started hunting, along with his two good friends, Roddy and Hugh Owens, who were as passionate about racing as he was. He was a natural and quickly gained a reputation.

Emma resigned herself to it, but vowed to support her son the best she could. She was joined in that endeavour by her daughters Emily and Alice, as well as by her loyal maidservant and housekeeper Molly, who had been with the family for years and who very clearly adored Fred. Not really knowing where else to turn, Emma often shared her concerns with her daughter Emily. Emily and Fred had always been really close and often spent any spare time huddled together discussing their life dreams. Emily wanted to be a teacher and Fred, of course, a jockey. As Fred's riding career progressed, Emily was becoming an invaluable sympathetic ear for Emma.

'Why is it only us ladies seem to see it?' Emma asked Emily on more than one occasion. 'Fred may have a talent, but I can see the demons he has to overcome within himself every time he climbs into the saddle. He'll push and push himself, but deep down inside he is insecure and unsure of his abilities. He'll be a winner, of that I am sure, but what will it cost him?'

Emily would nod and do her best to say the right thing. But what could she really say?

Emma knew her son better than anyone but, despite all his successes at everything equine, she could see what the constant pressure was doing to him. Even though Fred had the underdeveloped, whippet-thin body of a prepubescent boy, William was already lecturing him on keeping his weight down for racing. Emma hated to see Fred hesitating at the dinner table, fork raised to his mouth, looking nervously at his father. It didn't seem right that a growing lad should have to even think about things like that. Everything was just racing, racing, racing. That was certainly the case for William who appeared to think of little else. It was taking its toll in other areas too. There just never seemed to be enough money to go around.

Emma missed her father Bill greatly, since he was always such a wise source of counsel. She really needed someone to talk to about her fears for the future and once again she found herself turning to Emily.

'Well, my dear mother, I really do not know how to advise you on these matters,' Emily replied, after hearing her out. That day's hunt was just getting ready on the cobblestones outside and there were numerous muffled shouts, barks and yelps. Mother and daughter were sat together in the gloomy backroom of the Kings Arms, getting a short rest before the hectic afternoon of eating and drinking that inevitably followed the hunt.

'Father certainly spends more on betting and his horses than he earns in here, that's for sure. If we're lucky, the creditors will be kind to us because of Father's past glories. There's not many people that don't remember his win on Little Charlie, but I do think we need to accept that memory will not pay the bills forever. Is he expecting my brothers to earn enough to pay the bills through racing?'

Emma shrugged and then nodded.

'Maybe, yes, I think so. At least that is partly why he pushes them all so hard. William Junior is OK. He's older and he has always been more robust than Fred. And, Charles, well he is still so young. It's Fred he pushes hardest.

'They're all down the park morning and night, but most of their father's focus is on poor Fred. I worry about him, I really do. He is only ten. It's a lot of pressure to put on a little one. Then there is this thing with the bills, like I say. He's never had any thought on our books and how to make things pay.'

Emily leaned over and squeezed Emma's hand. Her eyes welled with tears.

'You mustn't worry so much, Mother, something will turn up.'

'I try not to,' Emma said, her voice barely a whisper now. 'I'll speak to him again, even though I know everything I say falls on deaf ears, particularly when it comes to Freddie. I just wish things were different.'

Emma had good reason to worry though. With five children all growing fast and horses that needed food and care, the Archer family needed a big break soon. Something needed to change, or they would be in big trouble in a matter of months. What she didn't count on was that the answer, when it came, would present one of the toughest choices she'd ever had to take.

A few weeks after the hunt, Emma was standing at the window of the Kings Arms when she saw her husband striding down the path, looking as proud as punch. When he caught sight of Emma, he waved her outside. Wondering what could be up, she walked slowly to the door, shooting Emily a nervous glance as she did so. Emily, who was sewing a coverlet, smiled back, but inwardly she felt nervous too. Something didn't feel right.

William was smiling broadly when she opened the door. Emma glanced around to see if Fred was with him and he obviously caught the look.

'He's with William Junior and Charlie, practising jumps.'

Of course he was, thought Emma. *Where else?*

'I've got to talk to you. I've got the most amazing news.'

Emma made her way to the stone bench that nestled under the sash windows at the back of the tavern yard and sat down. It was early autumn and the small back garden already looked bare and a little forlorn. The roses needed a final deadheading and the low hedge that separated the yard from the single-track road on the other side was starting to brown off at the edges. There was a definite chill in the air. Emily silently joined her, placing a protective hand on her shoulder.

'You know the La Terrière brothers?' William began. He was breathless and excited, not really expecting an answer from his wife.

Emma knew the La Terrières. They'd both raced as younger men and were still keen horsemen. William Junior and Fred, together with their friends Roddie and Hugh, got on well with the next generation of young La Terrières and they often went hunting together on the Cotswold Hunt. The La Terrière boys had a stable full of beautiful hunters but preferred the company of William and his friends so they could indulge in anything and everything to do with steeple-chasing and hunting.

'I was on my way back from the hunt and Dick La Terrière caught me up to have a chat,' William said, grinning broadly. Emma could see he was eager to get to the punchline, but equally wanted the satisfaction of telling his story to the full. She had an uneasy feeling about what one of the La Terrière brothers would want with William.

William ploughed on: 'He's like, "Oh, William, I wanted to have a talk with you." I asked him what I could do for him and he came right out with it. "What are your plans for Fred?" he says.'

Emma said nothing, fighting the knot that was growing in her stomach. She nodded to indicate her husband should go on. Emily squeezed her shoulder in silent understanding. Fred was always her favourite sibling.

'I told him I wasn't sure yet, but was pretty certain he had a good talent and the making of a jockey. It's well known the lad seems to have little fear on whomever he rides. That's when he says to me that "if I have no objection" he'd like to speak to his good friend Mat Dawson, who is a trainer in Newmarket. He reckons he might be keen to take him on as an apprentice. Can you believe it?'

Emma nodded, still unable to respond. William didn't seem to have noticed his wife had said nothing since she'd come outside. He had simply prattled on regardless.

'Well, you've heard of Mr Dawson, haven't you, Em? I met him a few years back when I was racing. He seemed to have some good horses and he is held in very high regard. It would be a wonderful opportunity for the lad.'

'Isn't Newmarket quite a long way away?' Emma began, at last finding her voice.

'Oh, it's only 100 miles or so,' William said, dismissively, as though it was but a short distance away.

'He seems so young,' Emma said quietly. 'He only celebrates his 11th birthday in January.'

'It's the perfect age. Just the same as me when I left home to start my career. In fact, it must be fate. Lord James always said this was exactly the break we needed for Fred.'

Emma caught her breath at the mention of Lord James. He'd been a close family friend since William's racing days and a regular visitor to the house. She pushed his name from her mind. Now was not the time for wistful memories. She had to focus because she was just about to lose her last hope of wrestling her son away from racing.

'William, Fred is not like you.' Emma gulped. 'He has such a gentle nature when not on the back of a pony and I fear that the rough boys of a large yard will bully him. It would distress me to think of that happening so far away.'

'Oh, don't be silly,' William said, dismissing her concerns with a wave of his large hand through the air as though he was batting them away. 'Mr Dawson has such a fine stable and many folk waiting to place their horses with him. I have heard that, although he is hard with the boys and horses alike, he treats them all with kindness. Fred will be safe there.'

'Can we just not tell Freddie until we know for sure? We don't want to get his hopes up and then...' Emma's voice faltered. This was her worst dream come true.

William agreed, albeit reluctantly, to keep the potential apprenticeship secret while letters were sent off and received, but he could barely disguise his impatience. The boys must have known something was up though because, after that, William pushed them harder than ever in training and Fred in particular. Fred was awarded even less respite than usual from the tough regime and his only relaxation was joking around with Molly, who he adored. She seemed to indulge young Fred just about as much as Emma and would even put up with him and his brothers' rough and tumble around the house, upsetting her careful housekeeping.

'You'll be the death of me, Fred Archer,' she'd giggle.

Fred would shoot back a cheeky grin and Molly would forgive him everything. Emma couldn't help noticing how charming her son was becoming, even at that tender age. If only his personality was given room to flourish, she mused.

William didn't have long to wait for news from Mat Dawson. His own reputation in the racing world after the Grand National win was such that a reply came back almost immediately. It said simply: *Send the boy along.*

'Send him?' William laughed gleefully, brandishing the precious letter in his large fist. 'I'll take him myself.'

Fred clearly had no idea what was about to happen when he was summoned to the parlour, along with the rest of the family and Molly.

'I have big news,' announced William proudly.

Emma sat in her chair, staring ahead, her hands gripped tightly together, her knuckles blanching. Emily had curled herself into a small ball at her feet.

'You've all probably heard of a very successful trainer called Mat Dawson? He's based in Newmarket. Well, he's asked Freddie here to come along to try out to be his apprentice.'

Fred looked stunned. His brown eyes, already quite large, were as big as saucers.

'What do you say, young Fred?'

'Thank you sir, I would love to serve my apprenticeship in Newmarket,' Fred said, beaming. Then, perhaps more quietly, he added, 'It does seem a long way from home.'

Emma bit her lip so hard a small droplet of blood fell onto her skirt. She could see behind the broad grin Fred had fixed upon his face for the benefit of his father. He looked lost already. How on earth was he going to cope without the comfort of home at such a young age?

She glanced Emily who had curled herself into an even tighter ball, her head hidden in her arms, and then she looked over at Molly who was looking at the floor. The housekeeper's shoulders were slumped, as though she wanted the ground to swallow her up. In an instant she understood her shock. Molly had come to them aged eleven too. There had been a most terrible house fire and both her parents and her younger sister had perished in the vicious flames. From a happy contented childhood, everything she knew had been ripped away in an instant. Emma had taken her in and loved her like a daughter, but the memory had burned a hole in her heart too. Molly had rebuilt her life, with the help and love of the Archer family, especially through her fondness of Fred who had just been born when she had arrived, but now she saw everything about to change again. The significance of Fred being aged eleven too, was not lost on her, just as it had rang alarm bells with Emma when she thought about William at the same age.

William was not in the mood for debate. Less so than ever, in fact.

Fixing his stare ahead he said firmly: 'I left home at the same age as you are now, Fred. I am sure if you get a place there will be plenty of boys the same as you. There is no need to worry on that score, lad.'

William was not a sentimental man by any means. Being one of thirteen children, it had never been much of a wrench to leave home and he certainly had no happy memories of his early family life. While William undoubtedly loved his children, he could never see past the fact horses would be their livelihood and that, above all else, was all that mattered. He even secretly hoped his girls would marry trainers. It was the only world he knew. He did, however, adore his wife and, although he wanted Fred to go, he was also sad Emma did not share his feelings. Despite his brash behaviour, he did value her opinion. He could never quite believe that she had agreed to marry him at all. He always marvelled at the interesting people she knew and wanted Fred to live a life like hers. This was his son's big opportunity. Why could no one see that?

'Mr Dawson says you can go in February, after your eleventh birthday,' he told Fred. 'How about that?'

'It's wonderful news, sir,' said Fred, doing a

remarkable job of appearing to brighten up. 'I feel very proud to have been asked.'

William smiled back in delight.

'I'll need to practise a lot more before I leave, won't I?' Fred said, warming to the idea now the initial shock had passed. 'How will I get there? Will I be able to take Moss with me?'

'Whoa, slow down my son,' said his father, lifting his hands in mock surrender at the barrage of questions. 'No, Moss will stay here, lad, and I will take you there. Mr Dawson says I may stay a couple of weeks to see that you are settled in. Mother, you must stop your fretting and put a smile on your sad face. I will not leave him there if it is not suitable.'

If Emma was unconvinced before, she'd have been even less so if she'd seen the wink William gave Fred as he said this. There would be no bringing the boy back home in William's eyes. If his son didn't like it, he'd need to toughen up pretty quick.

CHAPTER TWO

Emma loved it when the Kings Arms public house was closed. She could take time to write letters, or entertain guests in peace. Today, the parlour was warm and cosy. Candles flickered, casting a faint glow into the darkened room, and wood crackled in the hearth. Emma indicated to Lord James he should take the seat closest to the fire and he settled into it, his hands outstretched towards the warm flames. He had the gait of one who was comfortable and at home in his surroundings.

'Dear Emma, I had to call after I heard the news that Fred had left for Newmarket a few days ago,' Lord James said quietly, his face etched in concern. 'I had no idea it was happening this soon. How are you? Have you had any news on how he's settling in?'

Emma, settling into the chair opposite, shook her head sadly.

'No,' she replied. 'I have had no news. I'm sure all is well. William has gone with him and will be staying with the Dawsons for a week or two, so he is not completely alone.'

The room lapsed into silence, save for the occasional crackle and hiss of the fire. They both knew that William was not the best choice for looking after the emotional needs of a young boy who was nervous and unsure about his new situation.

Lord James had known the Archers for many years. He kept a fine stable and had been an early patron of William, relying heavily on his advice and counsel when it came to buying horses. He had often asked William to travel the length of the land to inspect a horse he was thinking of adding to his stables. Yet, while he respected William wholeheartedly, the reason for his frequent trips to the Kings Arms was now sitting in front of him.

Lord James had fallen for Emma from the moment he had first spied her. He'd come to the Kings Arms' yard to talk to William about a new horse and William had insisted his patron met his new young wife Emma. She'd stepped demurely out of the back door and the nobleman was utterly smitten.

He'd stepped forward, taken her hand and brushed his lips against it. He vaguely remembered muttering something clumsy about it being an honour, or something like that. He'd giggled to himself. It was not like him to be so gauche or tongue-tied, but he just couldn't help it.

Emma, sensing the electricity between them, had looked down feeling confused, a faint tinge of redness rising to her cheeks.

'The honour is all mine, sir,' she'd murmured, looking up through her long lashes at the tall, slim and dark-haired gentleman.

Although conversation was awkward at first, the two soon found they had a lot in common. They shared a passion for literature, the countryside and history. Emma knew it was wrong to compare, but she couldn't help wondering how wonderful her life would have been if she had married someone this intelligent, charming and inquisitive. It was too late now and wrong to even think it, even if they were not from two completely different classes, but it didn't stop her. Nor did it stop the venerable Lord James from similar imaginings.

If William noticed quite how much Lord James visited, he never said anything. Neither did he mention how often the pair used to take tea together in the parlour. Perhaps he was happy his wife had someone to talk to. Plus, he was also safe in the knowledge Molly was always close by, serving tea and stoking the fire.

As if on cue, Molly tapped on the door and, without waiting for an answer, hurried into the room. Emma smiled at her and her guest gave the housekeeper a friendly nod.

'Would His Lordship like some tea?'

'Well, that is very kind. I was not expecting to stay for very long, but that would be nice.'

'I'll be back shortly,' Molly replied, heading back to the door.

'Thank you Molly,' Emma said, as Molly gently closed the door behind herself.

'I am so pleased to see you again Edward, it's been

such a long while,' Emma said, turning her gaze back to her guest. Her voice tapered off as their eyes met. They both knew why it had to be a while. Each time it became more difficult.

Emma quickly looked away and grappled for safer ground.

'Freddie has grown into a truly charming young boy, with kindness and sensitive ways,' she began. 'I hope that in years to come he will be at an advantage, but alas I'm not sure that will be the case while he is in stable quarters alongside ten other boys. Perhaps I worry far too much, do you not think?'

Her companion smiled warmly.

'Emma, my dear, he will be all right. Mr Dawson is a fine trainer with a great family history with horses.'

'Everyone keeps telling me that, but I fear I know very little about him.'

'Well, then let me distract you by telling you more about Mr Mat Dawson.'

'You are good to me.'

'Not at all. It is to my own advantage to see a smile light up that pretty face of yours. I am being selfish really.'

Emma giggled, despite her sombre mood.

'Where to begin? Ah, yes. Mr Dawson comes from Gullane, which is up in Scotland, and his family boasts a long history of horsemen and trainers. His father, I believe, was one of the leading trainers north of the border and his three brothers have followed the family trade too.

'By all accounts, they are all well-mannered, have good stable management skills and their judgment of a yearling is second-to-none. Our Mr Dawson came south as a young man and, after a brief stint as a private trainer, where I understand he had some success for Lord John Scott, he set up as a public trainer in Newmarket on the Heath House estate.

'He's obviously doing something right because he has attracted some pretty well-to-do patrons. The Dukes of Hamilton, Portland, and Newcastle can't talk highly enough about him. Apparently, his attention to detail is unparalleled. He can time the training of a horse to a tee so they are in peak form right on the day of a race. Not many people in this country can do that. He's an impressive trainer. In fact, I've pretty much never heard a bad word spoken about him.'

'Pretty much?' pressed Emma, immediately leaping at the barely noticeable inference.

At that moment, the door opened and Molly came in carrying a tray. On it was a large tea pot, two bone china cups and saucers and a small plate of delicate finger cakes. She set the tray down on a side table and busied herself pouring tea. As she carefully placed a cup in front of each of the pair, along with a small plate for the cakes and the cakes themselves, Lord James continued.

'Ah, well that would be telling,' he chuckled.

'Well, you can't stop now,' Emma said, doing her best to sound equally light-hearted, but finding it difficult to hide the concern in her voice. Picking up her cup and taking a small sip of tea, she thanked

Molly and urged Lord James to continue.

'All right, all right. I've heard he has not lost any of that blunt outspokenness that is said to be common to all Scots. He is no respecter of birthrights, however high born his patrons.'

'And this manifests itself how?' Emma interrupted, feeling alarmed. How would her son cope with a gruff Scot? Surely it would be a case of out of the frying pan and into the fire after his experiences with William.

'Well, I did hear one funny story. Apparently, he really rather likes his Sunday afternoon nap. No one is allowed to disturb it on the threat of the biggest tongue-lashing they ever did get. The story goes that one noble owner of a string of horses Mr Dawson was looking after didn't quite understand that. Or, perhaps no one had thought to tell him. Either way, he turned up one Sunday and demanded to see "his" trainer. No amount of persuasion would get him to come back another day. He pretty much demanded to see Mr Dawson.'

'What happened?' Emma asked, eyes wide. She was enjoying the story, even though it was not helping her misgivings about Newmarket.

Lord James let out another huge chuckle as he delivered the punchline.

'Our Mr Dawson struggled downstairs and says to this nobleman: "You want to see your horses today? You can see them tomorrow too, when you take them away." They both laughed.

'Thank you for telling me about him,' Emma said, nodding thoughtfully. 'I'm most grateful. Although, I have to say, I am not sure it has made me feel much better. If Mr Dawson is so exacting, do you think he drives his apprentices too hard?'

'I'm sure he is probably a hard taskmaster, yes,' Lord James said gently. 'His horses probably need to stand up to some pretty tough preparation and so too, do his boys, I expect…'

Emma winced.

'…But I am equally sure it will be the making of young Fred. He just needs to settle in.'

She nodded sadly.

'I just wish I had some word on what was happening,' she said helplessly.

Word didn't come until three weeks later, by which time William had returned full of bluff and bluster about what an extraordinary stables Fred was working in. Her husband talked at length about the strict routines, how they were up at dawn mucking out and then working long into the night. Despite this toil, William was quite sure there were many, many would-be apprentices clamouring for this incredible opportunity. Yet, while Emma could now vividly picture the layout of the estate, thanks to William's intricate descriptions, she was still no nearer to knowing anything about her son. William simply could not be drawn on any details about Fred.

'He's fine, he's fine,' he replied to all Emma's entreaties. 'You can't wrap him in cotton wool all his life. This will make a man of him. Better still, it will make him a champion.'

It wasn't until Emma received a short note from

Fred a few days later that she got a small idea of what was really going on and all her worst fears were realised. The crumpled note was written in scrawled, semiliterate sentences, some of which were barely readable, but the sentiment was clear: Fred was desperately unhappy and homesick. Even more worryingly, he was being bullied mercilessly by the other, much older stable hands.

Emma thought her heart would break when she read his final sentence:

'Please, please let me come home.'

Of course, she went straight to William and pleaded and pleaded with him to end Fred's apprenticeship. And, of course, William wouldn't hear a word about it.

'But he is so unhappy,' she wailed.

'What does happiness matter?' William growled. 'It's your fault for treating him like a china doll. He needs to toughen up. I did. I don't see why he can't. He needs to prove himself.'

Emma knew whatever she said, her husband would not agree to release her Freddie from his obligations. She felt wretched and helpless as she sat down to pen a reply. Keeping her tone upbeat, she urged her son to stay strong.

'It will get easier my darling son,' she wrote. *'These things are always strange at first, but once the other boys get to know you as I do, they will like and respect you.'*

In an attempt to keep things upbeat and cheer him up, she wrote about news from home. There were little stories about the antics of Fred's brothers and sisters, details of the latest hunts and who was up to what in the village. She shared the exciting announcement that Molly was now engaged to Bert, who worked for the La Terrière family.

'Isn't it wonderful news?' she wrote. *'We're all dizzy with happiness and running around making all the arrangements. I shall certainly be writing to Mr Dawson to ask him to release you for the wedding.*

'In the meantime, I enclose a letter from Emily. She is so impatient to know how you are and won't rest till you reply.'

A few weeks later, Emma received a reply from her son, along with a note for his anxious sister Emily. While he was much cheered by Molly's impending wedding, he could report no respite in the bullying. Over a series of letters over subsequent weeks, Emma pieced together what was happening. Much of the time she had to read between the lines, because her son was not a skilled communicator, but she gradually built up a clearer picture.

The root of the problem was, as is so often the case, jealousy. The more experienced stable lads felt intimidated by William when he arrived to drop off Freddie. This was down to his success in the Grand National and also his rather immodest swagger. It certainly didn't help that the boss, Mr Dawson, seemed to favour William so highly: they naturally assumed he would feel the same about Fred.

Funnily enough, as Fred had astutely surmised quite early on, Mat Dawson was the last man in the world to show favouritism. He had strict rules on behaviour in the stable, which ran well above the usual ones for routine and discipline, although, admittedly, most of the rules were in favour of creatures with four legs! No horse was to be sworn at, or badgered by the lads, and the stick was not to be used without permission.

It was the accommodation arrangements that afforded poor Fred the most grief. While William had the honour of being accommodated in the Dawsons' main residence, he never got to experience the cramped quarters which the stable lads called home. Up to two dozen lads were packed into one long, barn-like room, their small, wooden beds stacked side-by-side along each wall like rows of coffins. The older boys set about intimating poor Fred right away, teasing him about his diminutive size. Then the tricks began. A constant favourite was to sneak up to Fred's locker while he was asleep, take all his clothes and throw them through the window. By the time he woke early the next day and discovered they were gone (again) he'd dash outside to find them in the yard below, soaked in rain and mud. He'd have no alternative but to wear them, because he had no other clothes. Then, as well as being cold and wet, he'd also be in trouble for his slovenly appearance. Hardly surprisingly, poor Fred was in tears nearly each morning before he rode out.

There were constant verbal threats too. Mr Dawson had strict rules about not leaving the sleeping accommodation at night and the house and stables were surrounded by a stiff wire fence to emphasise the point. Of course, boys being boys, the apprentices had discovered a route out many years before. The secret of the route out was handed down from generation to generation of stable lads and fiercely guarded. The older boys were certain to make it clear to Freddie there would be severe consequences if he blabbed to Mr Dawson they were all enjoying nights out. Fred wasn't stupid. He never said a word. He was too scared anyway.

Emma couldn't help but notice Fred did not blame the rough boys for their actions. When he wrote about them in his letters he would frequently say he didn't think it was their fault.

'Many of the other lads have not been lucky enough to come from a family like ours, which is why they don't understand or care for others,' he wrote. *'They believe that to get anywhere you have to fight for it and that's what they do best.'*

Emma was relieved when Fred wrote to say he had finally made some friends. Two young lads called Joe and Sam, who started at the stables a few years earlier, took it upon themselves to look after the lonely figure. Joe was especially kind and would lend Fred dry clothes whenever his were found in a sodden heap below the window.

'Joe tells me I have to pretend I don't care,' Fred wrote to his mother. *'He says it's hard but 'tis the only way. Joe's been here a few years now and says while they are a bit rough it does get easier in time. He went through the same but it did stop. He promised me it would stop for me too.'*

Slowly, very slowly, Fred's letters seemed to become happier. Or, if not exactly happy, certainly less sad. He stopped asking to be brought home. Reading between the lines, as she always did, Emma detected a grudging respect growing for Fred among his compatriots. Although most people could see that her son was nervous, delicate, perhaps even highly strung, it was equally obvious he was very different in character when he got near a horse. In fact, he was gaining a reputation for being prepared to get up on, and master, any mount regardless of how difficult they were.

His reputation was growing outside of Mat Dawson's yard too.

It was William Archer that brought home this news. He'd been on a trip to inspect a horse in Cambridge for the La Terrière brothers and could barely contain himself the moment he burst through the door.

'Em, Em! Girls, you've got to hear this,' he shouted, slamming the heavy front door behind him.

Emma and her daughters popped their heads out of the kitchen, looking perplexed. When they saw the broad grin on William's face they too broke out into smiles.

'Hello William,' laughed Emma. 'What on earth has got you so excited? Honestly, you gave us all such a shock.'

'Ha, well, I have news you see. News about Fred.'

Emma caught her breath and then reassured herself it must be good news or her husband wouldn't be so cheerful.

'Well, perhaps you would be so good as to share it with us then?' Emma said.

Her daughters added their voices in encouragement. Emily had been writing to her favourite brother every weekend.

'For a tankard of beer perhaps?' teased William, who really was in unusually good spirits.

'Molly, would you bring William some beer please? Shall we go to the parlour?'

The Archer family poured into the parlour and William settled into his favourite chair.

'When I was in Cambridge, I ran into this newspaper man,' he began, almost breathless in his haste to tell the story. 'John Corlett, the owner and editor of *The Sporting Times*, you know, the "Pink 'Un"?'

The ladies all nodded. Everyone was familiar with the pink newspaper so beloved by race-goers. They just wanted him to get to the point though!

'Well, we got to talking and when he found out who I was, he says: "Are you the father of Fred Archer?" I am, says I, the one and same. "The Fred Archer that rides for Mat Dawson?" Indeed I am, says I.

'"Now there is a lad," he says. I asked him how he knew him and it turned out he had not long come from Dawson's stables. Apparently, Dawson pointed straight at our Fred and said, "I shall make a jockey out of that lad someday." He tells the newspaper man that our Fred is the pluckiest lad he ever had. He'd do anything.'

Emma smiled. She was pleased her son was doing so well, but at the same time she didn't want him doing anything reckless.

'Fred was riding a bay horse called St Pancras, which was being trained for the flat. Dawson shouts him over and tells him to ride it over the fence into the next field. John Corlett says Dawson's exact words were: "Your father used to ride over fences and I don't see why you shouldn't." Anyway, Fred did just that and then jumped straight back over again. He didn't question it, or belly ache about it, saying the horse wasn't up to it. He just went straight out and did it. That newspaper man said he never saw anything like it.'

Alice and Emily clapped their hands and, despite her reticence over Fred's new life, Emma felt quite proud too.

'Did he tell you anything else?' she urged.

'A little. He said that Mr Dawson told him that Fred was always the first out to the yard and the last one to finish. He is always checking and wanting to know everything about the new horses that arrive. You see Em, I was right. He's all right and he's doing a great job too.'

Emma couldn't help agree that it sounded that way, but felt she couldn't be certain until Fred returned the following month to attend Molly's wedding. Then she'd be sure.

In the days before Fred came home, Emma couldn't settle. She must have checked his room a dozen times, making and re-making his bed until it was just so. She'd given Molly strict instructions to make her son all his favourite treats.

'He'll be watching his weight,' growled her husband. 'You're spoiling him again.'

'Oh, don't be silly. A little cake won't do any harm. Besides, I bet he hasn't eaten properly in months.'

On the day he was due, Emma was up at the crack of dawn to check everything all over again and then kept glancing outside to see if she could spot the little cart that would be bringing her son home from the station. She was nearly exhausted with anticipation by the time he arrived in the late afternoon.

'Freddie!' she shrieked, running to the door, followed closely by his four siblings and Molly.

They opened the door and all stopped at once. The small skinny boy that had left the house not six months before, had changed completely. He was still unbearably slim, but he was now tall and looked like, well, a young man.

'Hello Mother,' he grinned.

Emma gasped. His voice had broken and he even sounded completely different.

'Young William, Charles, girls. Gosh, how you have all changed.'

'Not as much as you,' said William Junior, darting forward. He took Fred's hand and pumped it up and down in a warm handshake.

'You're so tall,' giggled Alice, running forward to give him a hug.

'Yes,' agreed Emily, throwing herself into the fray and wrapping herself around both her sister and Fred. 'You look like you've been stretched in a mangle.'

'That's why he is still so skinny,' laughed Charles, patting him on the shoulder.

'That is enough, all of you,' chided Emma. 'Get away from him and let him have room to breathe.'

Her children stepped back respectfully and Emma took a few paces forward. Gathering up each of

Fred's hands in her own, she looked searchingly into his face. It was still her Fred, but he looked different somehow. He was definitely older and more mature, but there seemed to be a great sadness about him too. He looked almost lost.

'Are you all right?' she said quietly.

'Yes, I am now,' he smiled back, his dark brown eyes shining. He was undoubtedly pleased to see his mother. 'And things are much better for me now too. You can stop worrying.'

'Good. Now, I want you to come in and tell us all about it.'

With William out working, the throng headed towards the kitchen and settled around the table there. The informal setting seemed just right to hear all about Fred's adventures. The girls busied themselves making tea and laying out cakes, while Emma and the boys settled into chairs around the large, worn oak table.

'Where shall I start?' Fred said, feeling a little self-conscious to be the centre of attention.

'At the beginning, stupid,' laughed William Junior.

Emma flashed a reproachful look at her eldest son.

'Just tell us what you do every day,' she said. 'And tell me about Mr Dawson.'

'It is much as I wrote in my letters. We start very early each day and we have a pretty busy workload getting horses ready for races. There is a lot going on, so Mr Dawson expects you to know what to do. He wouldn't have it if you were asking him what to do all the time. He's got a sixth sense for weaklings, or rogues, and they have to leave the stables pretty quickly.

'After the horses have their breakfasts each day, their owners may come and see them, but not always. Sometimes they just want to talk to Mr Dawson about a race to hear about their horse's chances.

'I ride every day, sometimes twice and it is always different horses. Mr Dawson says I am good with the highly strung ones, so I often get the difficult ones. He reckons I will be good enough to race for him next spring.'

Emma noticed her son's cheeks colour slightly as he said this, but he also looked proud.

'Don't you get any time off?' asked Emily, plonking herself down in a chair noisily.

'Yes, sometimes. Joe, Sam and I go into Newmarket together and wander around, if we get the chance, but it doesn't happen often.'

'Well, you've got a few days off now, so let's make the most of it,' smiled Emma.

'Not a few days, Mother,' her son smiled back. 'Mr Dawson says I can have two whole weeks off.'

'You never told me!' shouted Emma, leaping to her feet in the excitement.

Fred's sisters were also shrieking and for a few moments the room descended into mayhem.

'I wanted it to be a surprise,' Fred said, when he could finally get a word in. 'Now, where is the bride to be? Will I get to see her before the wedding tomorrow?'

The next 24 hours were a flurry of excitement and arrangements. The Kings Arms vibrated to the noise of laughter and shrieks as the Archer children ran around getting everything ready for Molly's big day. Even William lost his normally gruff exterior and joined in with all the practical jokes and tricks being played by each member of the family. Emma couldn't have been happier either. Everyone was together and now she could see first-hand that her son was safe and well and, at least, happy enough. She still wasn't sure that racing was the career she wanted for him, but if he was content, then that was as much as she could ever hope for.

By the time they finished, the rooms in the Kings Arms looked breathtakingly beautiful. They'd been decorated with a brightly coloured combination of dried flowers, holly berries and pretty ribbons. The dining table almost groaned with food and each dish was so beautifully presented it looked good enough for the King. There were whole joints of cold meat, delicately flavoured pies, with thick pastry crusts, plus a range of cheeses, vegetables, breads and pickles. Alongside it all was a feast of richly coloured cakes and tarts.

Molly stayed with the Archers on the morning of her wedding and Fred was given the honour of driving the pony and trap that would take her to the church. While everyone had been fussing over the inside of the house, the young horseman had been polishing the trap until it gleamed. He had put the ribbons that Alice and Emily had made in the pony's mane and tail, and hung a little bell off the whip stand. Emma had put a warm blanket on the seat as, even though it was September, it still might get cold later in the day. Fred was similarly well turned out. In fact, his riding boots were so clean and shiny, Emma joked she could almost see her reflection in them.

When Molly appeared at the bottom of the stairs in a simple satin dress, trimmed with delicate lace and set off with a tiara of dried flowers woven into her hair, Emma gasped. She looked exquisite.

'Molly, you are so beautiful,' said Emma, her hand on her heart. 'Bert is going to be so happy.'

Tears of happiness were falling down the bride's cheeks.

'Oh mistress, how can I ever thank you for such a wonderful wedding? You and the master have been so kind.'

'Come now Molly, you've been like a daughter to us. We'd have it no other way. Now, stop those tears, you'll make your face all blotchy. Besides, we've got no time for this. We've only got half an hour to get to the church.'

Emma hugged Molly and opened the door to the hall where the whole family stood waiting in a line. They were a wonderful picture. Even William had put on a clean shirt and jacket.

At 1pm, Molly came out of the front door looking radiant. Freddie was so happy to see her in the wonderful dress and veil. He helped Molly up onto the gig, placed the blanket over her knees and then climbed up himself.

He turned to her and smiled.

'You look so pretty.'

Molly smiled back and squeezed his arm affectionately.

'Thank you, Freddie. That means the world to me. I'm so happy you could be here today and thank you so much for taking me to the church. Now, let's be on our way or Bert will be worrying I've changed my mind.'

The pretty little gig set off down the lane towards Molly's new future.

The wedding went so well it was talked about in the village in awed tones for years to come. The guests marvelled at the richness of the feast, the seemingly endless supply of free-flowing ale and the dancing which went on, on the lawn, until late in the night.

Emma was so happy for Molly and she was also delighted to see Fred so relaxed among his friends and family. For the first time she began to hope things would be all right. Looking at him then, laughing and joking with Roddy and Hugh Owen, she had the glimpse of the man he could be.

'You shouldn't be standing all alone on the sidelines,' said a low voice beside her, stopping her daydream with a start.

Emma span around and came face to face with Lord James. Lord James had been staying with the La Terrière family for the weekend and William, who had been doing some work for the La Terrières, had invited him to come along and give Molly and Bert his good wishes.

'Lord James,' she gasped. 'You startled me.'

'Edward,' he signed, with a teasing smile. 'You

could at least call me Edward when we are alone.'

'We're not alone,' laughed Emma. 'There must be 100 guests here.'

'And you think they are looking at us? They are all looking at the beautiful bride, or fawning over your child prodigy.'

'You really are the living end,' Emma teased back. Her eyes shone and she felt a little giddy. She wasn't sure if it was the ale, or Edward James. He always made her feel a little off kilter.

'But he is all right, isn't he?' he said, sounding serious. 'Like I said? He looks cheered anyhow.'

'Yes, he is fine,' Emma said, staring at her son.

'There you go. Five years of an apprenticeship will pass by in a flash and he'll be home again, getting under your feet.'

'Five years just feels like a lifetime though,' Emma sighed.

She could feel Lord James shifting himself, so there was barely any space between them. As he did so, his hand brushed oh so gently against hers.

'If you get your heart's desire at the end of it, you can withstand a lifetime of waiting,' he whispered.

She could almost feel his breath on her bare neck. Tearing herself away, she wiped her moist palms on the side of her dress and cleared her throat.

'I had better go and check that we're not running out of ale,' she said, matter-of-factly and headed off to the back door of the inn at a brisk pace.

She didn't look back. She knew she should not and

reproached herself for flirting with Lord James again. She'd surely go to hell, or be cursed if she behaved in such a wanton way again. To force herself back to reality, she glanced over at Fred. He was still engrossed in conversation.

He's my priority, she thought. *It doesn't matter how talented everyone says he is, I need to keep him safe.*

CHAPTER THREE

The day before Fred left to return to Heath House, he sought out Emma mid-afternoon. He knew his mother was still fretting and often caught her scrutinising him when she thought he was not looking. Fred wanted to put her mind at ease.

After a brief search, he found her in the parlour, in front of the fire sewing.

'Ah, I thought I would find you here,' he said, settling into a chair beside her.

'Oh, Freddie, you startled me. I was miles away. Is there anything you need?'

'No, no, not at all. As you know, I am going tomorrow, so I just wanted to spend a little time with you.'

'That is so thoughtful of you,' said Emma, putting down her embroidery and giving his arm a squeeze. 'Are you excited about going back?'

'I think so, yes. It is a lot better now. The older lads mainly leave me alone and if any do speak to me, it is often to ask my advice. I take that as a good sign.'

'They know how talented you are.'

'That is very kind, but I had a good teacher in Father.'

'Even though he pushed you so hard?'

Fred paused for a moment.

'He only wanted what was best for me,' he said at last. 'Just as Mr Dawson does.'

'But you do like Mr Dawson?' Emma said anxiously.

'I do. In fact I like both Mr and Mrs Dawson. Mr Dawson is strict, but fair and can be very kind if he is pleased with you. His wife is very kind also and really looks out for us lads. It's her you should be thanking for all those letters I've been writing. She makes sure we all go up to their house and write one every Sunday, without fail. I don't mind that. I used to struggle with my writing, but it is getting easier. Besides, Mrs Dawson always slips an extra piece of cake into my pocket when I am on the way out.'

Emma made a mental note to thank Mrs Dawson when she met her. She liked the sound of this kind woman.

At his mother's encouragement, Fred described his favourite horses and daily routine. She had never heard Freddie talk so much and after nearly an hour of hearing his stories, she felt so much better. It was nice to laugh and joke with her son. There was a time she feared he would never seem so light-hearted, nor her, for that matter.

'Freddie, it all sounds well with you,' she said at

long last, as the shadows began to grow long across the parlour. 'I am not going to worry so much any more. I'm sure it's not all gone away, but I will certainly sleep better after our talk.'

'Thank you, Mother. I am so glad you feel less concerned. Right now, I had better go and get my things ready and start saying my goodbyes. I have to be off early tomorrow morning.'

The pair stood up and hugged. Emma gulped back the sobs that were rising in her throat. She didn't want her son to know how sad she felt at seeing him go again. Luckily Fred didn't seem to notice. He gave her one last squeeze and started to make for the door.

'Oh, I almost forgot to say, Lord James called at Heath House to see Mr Dawson,' Fred said, just as he was about to leave the room. Emma started in surprise to hear the mention of Edward's name in such a strange context. She checked herself and bade her son to continue.

'I was called up to the house to see him and he asked about my apprenticeship and how I was faring. It was a good few months ago now. It was good to see him again. I still remember him watching me go round the orchard on my donkey, although that feels a long time ago now.

'He was very generous and brought me a pair of leather gloves and a food parcel. All the lads were very envious, but I shared it with them. Strangely enough, that is when the teasing and tricks really slackened off, so maybe the cake helped.

'Anyway, I thought I would tell you and, don't worry, I did write to him to say thank you.'

Emma smiled.

'Oh Freddie, you read my mind, that is exactly what I was going to say. I'm glad you wrote to Lord James. How very kind of him to call. Now off you go and I will see you later.'

As Freddie shut the door behind him, Emma was pensive. She couldn't help wondering if Lord James' visit was more than to pass on some comforting gifts. It would be so like him to have a quiet word with Mr Dawson about the bullying problem after hearing her concerns. Edward was so charming, the stable proprietor would probably have been putty in his hands. It certainly wasn't completely impossible that someone had quietly warned the older lads to leave her son alone. Even if Edward hadn't gone this far, his generosity had certainly played a part in calming the situation. For that, Emma was eternally grateful.

The following day, after numerous heartfelt goodbyes, Fred returned to Heath House. When he arrived he discovered it in a great state of excitement. While he had been away, Lord Falmouth had paid Mat Dawson a visit and asked him to do the same in return, coming to see his stud at Mereworth Castle, in Kent. The gentleman, who had come into the title of sixth viscount Falmouth quite unexpectedly through the early death of a cousin, was a quiet, unassuming and intelligent man. He'd got on with Mat Dawson immediately, reciprocal visits were made and in no time at all an agreement was struck to send his horses to Heath House.

The news didn't take long to filter out into the stables where the lads were grooming and sorting out the tack room. One of the newer lads, Jamie, raced across the yard to tell everyone as soon as he overheard it.

'Lord Falmouth is bringing his horses here,' he said, still panting from his exertions and yet proud to be able to break this interesting news. 'I overheard Mr Dawson tell Mrs Dawson in the kitchen.'

A great cheer went up among the lads at almost the exact moment Fred arrived in the yard.

'What's up?' he said, coming to a halt by his good friend Joe and setting his bag down on the cobblestones.

'It seems Lord Falmouth is the newest nobleman to bring us his horses,' Joe said, clapping Fred heartedly on the back by way of greeting. 'The lads are pretty pleased because, by all accounts, he has a string of very good horses.'

Fred nodded thoughtfully. That was good news indeed.

'Well Freddie, my lad, if we play our cards right we will be getting some good rides in the future, that's for sure. I bet the master is well chuffed with the news.'

'I would say so, indeed. I'm definitely going to put that in my next letter home. Father will be delighted.'

Fred ran off to put his things down before he got to work cleaning bridles. All the while, his mind was racing with the possibilities. Mr Dawson had already indicated his first race was not far off, so perhaps he might get an opportunity even sooner with such a burgeoning stable. He certainly felt ready. More than ready, in fact. He just wanted to prove himself.

Luckily, Fred did not have long to wait and he was right in his assumption this was good news for him. The Heath House stables were gaining a better reputation by the day and with growing numbers of fine horses to train and look after, Mat Dawson was more keen than ever to match them with top quality apprentices. With one eye on the future, he decided it was time to take Fred to the next stage of his training.

At that time, Fred Webb was Heath House's nominated lightweight jockey. To give Fred Archer some experience, Mat Dawson decided to enter both of them into the Newmarket Second October meeting. Fred Webb was to ride Lord Falmouth's Stromboli, while his more junior stable-mate was to ride a mare called Honoria.

When Mr Dawson approached Freddie in the paddock to tell him about the plan, the young apprentice could barely contain his excitement.

'Oh, Mr Dawson, I'm so pleased,' he said. 'This will be my first race at Newmarket. I must write to tell my parents. I promised I would let them know because my mother really wanted to watch me.'

Fred was smiling broadly at Mr Dawson. The stable owner smiled back. He had such high hopes for this lad, but he also had to keep him in check.

'Well lad, I would wait a while before getting them to come and see you race,' he said, doing his best to ignore the disappointed expression on Fred's face. 'With Webb on Stromboli, you'll be doing the running. He's the experienced rider, after all. Do you not think it would be best for your parents to watch when there's a better chance you'll be near the front over the winning line?'

Fred straightened himself up and resumed his smile.

'Yes, of course,' he said. 'You are quite right. I'm sure that is a better plan. I had not thought of that and got a bit carried away by the thought of my first race at Newmarket. I hope you will forgive me, sir.'

'There is nothing to forgive. You've got a great career ahead of you, young Fred, as long as you keep your wits about you.'

'May I go and tell Joe and Sam? I'm sure they will be keen to come and watch me.'

Mat nodded and smiled. He was pleased to see that Fred had a level head on his shoulders. He'd always thought that to be the case.

'Of course, off you go.'

As Mat Dawson watched the young lad turn and run off back to the yard, he was conscious that the other apprentices would have been watching them talk, eager to know what was going on. Rivalry between the boys was intense and they all watched the master like a hawk to see who he was favouring. Keeping his facial expression as blank as possible, he turned to go back to the house. If anyone had looked closely though, they would have seen a gleam of almost fatherly pride in his eyes.

Mat Dawson and his wife were never blessed with children. It would be too simplistic to say he felt like Freddie was his son. He cared deeply for most of his apprentices. There was something special about this boy though. He respected his abilities and also liked his gentle, sensitive, almost vulnerable temperament. It brought out protective instincts he hadn't realised he had. He knew his wife adored Fred too and he made a great show of chiding her not to 'spoil' the boy, even though he was probably just as guilty as she was of looking out for him. They both just knew though: this lad was special.

Joe and Sam were really pleased for Fred when he told them the news. They'd both been racing for a year and it was nice to hear the youngster was finally getting his chance too.

It turned out both boys had rides scheduled in Newmarket that day too, so all three would be at the races.

'We will be cheering you on to the post Freddie,' laughed Sam.

'You're gonna make us proud and beat that Fred Webb I hope,' added Joe.

'That's the plan,' said Fred.

The boys could see he was deadly serious. Ever since losing that day in the orchard, Fred had made a silent vow not to be beaten again. He really, really, didn't like losing.

In the days leading up to the race, Fred was out at work for more hours than ever before. If he was not riding, he was cleaning stables, checking horses and going through kit. His expression was fixed and deadly serious, he was so focussed on the race.

He asked anyone who would listen for advice on this or that and would quickly argue the toss if he didn't agree. Most people didn't seem to mind, but one or two of the older lads wondered what he was making all the fuss about.

'It's not like he is the first apprentice ever to ride, y'know,' they sniggered behind his back.

On more than one occasion, Fred sought out Mat to ask his advice on Honoria. He wanted to know everything he could about the mare.

Mat Dawson answered his questions truthfully, doing his best not to dampen his apprentice's enthusiasm, but was quite open in his opinions. 'She's a good horse, but I'm not sure about her form,' he said. 'My view is she may well go out hard, but not be up to the strong finish you'll need against such an experienced line-up.'

Fred nodded, barely mumbling a response. He was too fixated on working out his strategy.

'Just look on it as a great experience to get you used to racing conditions on a real course,' his master urged.

Mat Dawson's words fell on deaf ears. Fred was not going for an experience. He was going to win.

The day of the race itself was cold and wet. A thick carpet of autumn leaves covered the lanes around the racetrack and the strong wind that blew that day seemed to be able to do nothing to shift them.

After all his preparation of body and soul, young Fred was oblivious to the weather, even as the wind and rain whipped at his bare face as he rode down the course to the starting post. He already knew that, for the rest of his days, the racecourse was the one place where he felt completely at home and in control.

There was not an ounce of nervousness or fear in his body. He went over and over his race plan in his head: go out fast to take the lead, forcing others to follow at a quick pace.

As soon as the starter's flag went down, that is exactly what he did. The plan went beautifully and Honoria felt like she was flying beneath him. He felt almost weightless. He didn't let up, driving the mare on, acutely aware of the thunder of hooves close behind, waiting for him to make a mistake. But he wouldn't, because this was what he trained for. On and on he urged his mount. The course was swallowed up in his wake. He passed the halfway mark, still comfortably ahead and within moments was hurtling towards the three-quarter way marker.

Then, suddenly, inexplicably, Honoria ran out of steam. She seemed to stall, spluttering to a slow canter. In a split second, his opponents seized their advantage and surged past him. Fred felt like his heart was split in two. He dug his heels in and whipped the mare, hoping against hope he had got it wrong and she still had something left in her. But, she didn't. It was all gone. She was a spent force.

He heard the roar of the crowd as Fred Webb crossed the line, a comfortable few lengths ahead. He'd won for Lord Falmouth and the crowd loved it. The disappointment felt by his defeated opponent was almost unbearable. Poor Freddie Archer could barely face himself, let alone the crowds in the enclosure. The ride back there was unbearable.

'Freddie, Freddie, over here!' called Joe and Sam, almost simultaneously.

The pair grabbed Honoria's reins and Freddie jumped down, barely able to look his friends in the eye.

'What a race,' Joe said. 'I've never seen a start like it.'

'Shame about the finish though,' said Freddie glumly. 'She just run out of steam. I thought I had it, I really did. I was right out in front. Didn't you see?'

'Don't be daft,' said Sam, clapping him on the back. 'Didn't you hear the crowd roaring for you? They loved you. You've notched up a few fans today, that's for sure.'

Freddie smiled back at his friends.

'I guess it wasn't bad for a first race, was it?'

'That's the spirit,' agreed Joe. 'Oh, here comes the master now. He's smiling too.'

'Fred?' said Mat Dawson, looking from his protégé to Honoria, checking them both over.

'That was a good race. Well done. You did better than any of us could have hoped for. Don't reproach yourself.'

Freddie brightened.

'I heard from your father today,' Mat added. 'He's coming to see you later this week. I think he will be very pleased when he hears about this race.'

Freddie was already feeling a lot better. The pain of defeat still stung, but at least he hadn't disgraced himself. He'd run a good race, well, for the first three quarters of it, at any rate.

'Thank you sir. I am pleased I have made my first race, although I will be glad when I'm finishing first not last.'

'Oh that will be soon lad, I'm sure,' Mat said, smiling fondly at the lanky lad with the sad eyes and cheeky grin.

The following Tuesday, William Archer arrived at Heath House as expected and went straight to see Mr Dawson. As far as Fred knew, his father was dropping in on his way to a horse sale. However, the real purpose of William's visit was to find out more about his son's prospects. William's money problems were not getting any easier and creditors were becoming impatient. He was impatient to know if the time and faith he'd invested in his son was going to bear fruit any time soon.

William was delighted to hear about Fred's first race at Newmarket, but found it hard to conceal his disappointment at the result.

'But you reckon he'll get better,' he urged Mat Dawson. 'That boy has talent. I've always said it.'

'That is undoubtedly the case,' agreed Mat. 'We can't push him too hard though, not at this stage. I've seen dozens of apprentices come and go. You've got to take it one step at a time.'

All William's instincts pointed towards pushing the boy hard, but he had to respect the trainer. Mat Dawson's reputation was second to none. He just had to be patient. He just wasn't so sure his creditors would be so understanding.

'I understand you are going to the sale of Mr Naylor's horses,' said Mat, trying to move the conversation forward. 'You got your eye on something nice?'

'It so happens I have.'

'Why don't you take Fred along with you? He's worked so hard lately, he's due a day off. If you go over now, you are bound to find him in the yard.'

'That is very kind of you, I'll do just that,' nodded William.

Fred was pleased to see his father, even though it was just a few weeks since Molly and Bert's wedding. Although he was finally settling into Heath House, he was still homesick. William was equally pleased to see his son. While not an overly emotional man, he was still immensely proud of Fred and felt a great deal of affection for him.

After a brief chat in the yard, where Fred introduced his friends Joe and Sam to William, father and son set off to the horse sale. As they rode along the lane, William made his son go through the race almost step by step, to tell the story of how it went. Fred was pleased to oblige and didn't object whenever William cut in to clarify who was where and when and what he knew about this or that.

At the end of the tale, William nodded in satisfaction.

'Well my son, it sounds like you did all you could do and a little bit more. I am proud of you.'

They rode on in silence with Fred grinning broadly, his eyes shining. He was now more fired up than ever to do something even more spectacular in his next race.

The horse sale was in full swing when they arrived. There must have been a hundred or so men there, crowding around, both spectators and buyers. The air was filled with a cacophony of shouting, cheers and claps. Men were waving cloth hats in the air and gesticulating wildly as they discussed form. Many gripped full tankards of frothy ale, despite the early hour. Horses were led around in a specially set-off area and bidding was fierce.

William set off to find the horse he was supposed to be inspecting and left Fred to his own devices for a while. Fred loved horse sales. The sights, sounds and smells were so familiar to him. He'd known little else since the time he could first walk. The youngster knew plenty of people there too, many of whom stopped to speak to him.

After a leisurely circuit of the area, Fred ran right back into his father.

'Ah, speak of the devil, here he is now,' William boomed.

He had a tankard of ale in one hand and was standing beside a small, neatly turned out lady, with unfashionably short hair. She stood out in the crowd as one of the few ladies at the event and because of her rather manly dress.

'Freddie, you remember Mrs Wilan, don't you?'

Fred smiled and bobbed his head.

'Of course I do. How are you, madam?'

'My, hasn't he grown?' exclaimed Mrs Wilan.

The Archers had known Mrs Wilan for many years. She was a prominent racing figure with horses in training both on the flat and over fences. She held her own in the male-orientated world of horse racing, even earning the, albeit grudging, respect of most of her contemporaries. She seemed to take it all in her stride, and seemed to relish her nickname 'Croppy' on account of her rather short hair.

'Mrs Wilan was asking my advice on a good lightweight jockey,' William said, giving Fred a not-too-subtle nod.

Fred opened his mouth to respond, but his father couldn't bear the suspense and immediately broke back in.

'If you are looking for someone to ride your steeplechasers, madam, I have the very one to ride over fences for you. I'm sure Mr Dawson will give permission.'

His stubby finger pointed straight at Fred and he turned his gaze expectantly to Mrs Wilan.

'Why William, I'd be delighted to use your lad. If he's as good as you, I will undoubtedly have a winner in Bangor!'

William turned to Fred who was looking a little stunned at his sudden change in fortunes.

'Mrs Wilan has been looking for a lightweight to ride her pony, Maid of Trent, in the steeplechase at Bangor.'

'I'd really be honoured, madam,' Fred managed to stammer out at last.

'Perfect,' she said, clapping her hands. 'Leave it to me and I will visit Mr Dawson in the week and ask him.'

After saying her goodbyes, she plunged back into the crowd to continue her business.

'Well son? What do you think? There's just three weeks to prepare. Do you think you are ready for it?'

'Yes sir. I'll win this time too.'

'Good. You must train hard and have no distractions.'

'Absolutely.'

William took a long draught of his ale and smiled to himself. This was more like it, he thought. Out of the corner of his eye, he caught Fred nervously fidgeting. Then he cleared his throat.

'Father, I know you said no distractions, but I wonder if you would bring Mother and the girls to watch. Maybe Bert and Molly too? I promised them all they could come to my first race and well, it was probably just as well they didn't, but I'd like them to be there at this one.'

William looked thoughtful.

'Aye, of course,' he said. 'It's a few weeks away and if you give me your word you'll give them a good show, I'll get them there. How's that?'

'Very kind, thank you sir. I won't let you down. I promise.'

Fred could hardly wait to get started.

True to her word, Mrs Wilan visited Heath House the next day to ask if Freddie would be allowed to ride. Mat agreed straight away. He wanted his young protégé to get as much experience as possible. Everything was set for Fred Archer's first steeplechase race.

While Fred was characteristically focussed on the task ahead, preparations for the meet at Bangor started to generate a bit of a party atmosphere, both at the Kings Arms and Heath House. Perhaps inspired by William Archer's almost childlike enthusiasm, or maybe it was Fred's steadfast determination, Mat Dawson decided he would also make the trip to see Fred in action. Mrs Dawson said she'd like to go too and then Mat's brother John, who lived close by, chimed in that he wouldn't mind coming along either. In a matter of hours the entourage grew to include both sets of Mr and Mrs Dawsons, as well as John Dawson's ten-year-old daughter Helen.

As the flurry of preparations escalated, Mat Dawson said, as much to himself as to anyone else: 'Let us hope this race will be a success, with everyone making such a fuss. It's a good pony, that Maid of Trent, so I think Fred stands a good chance.'

By the day of the race itself, the festive atmosphere showed no signs of abating. While William Archer was desperate to go and visit Fred in the enclosure, to give him some last-minute instructions, Emma absolutely insisted he introduce her to the Dawsons before he did anything else. William opened his mouth to ask his wife to hang on, but was instantly quietened by the look she shot at him.

'Oh, come on then, I can see them just over there,' he growled, leading his wife and their small entourage across to the group of Dawsons.

'Mr Mat Dawson, Mrs Mary Rose Dawson, Mr John Dawson, and Mrs Grace Dawson, this is my wife Mrs Emma Archer,' William said, speaking at a rapid pace.

Emma and Mary Rose exchanged glances and giggled. They both understood how clumsy William could be in social situations at the best of times, but his impatience to get away on that day made him more abrupt than ever.

As always, Emma stepped in and, with her impeccable manners and grace, rescued the situation.

'I have waited for this moment so long,' she said quietly, stepping forward to greet Mat Dawson first. 'Mr Dawson, Freddie has told me so much about you. I am so grateful for your kind treatment of my son.'

'Mrs Dawson, it is so lovely to meet you. I can't say how thankful I am for all you have done for Freddie. You are so good making them write those letters home. They are a God-send, I tell you.'

Mary Rose and Emma both knew they would get along straight away. To spare any more awkwardness, Mary Rose stepped in to do the introductions properly, steering Emma to her brother-in-law and then sister-in-law and soon the group were all chatting like old friends. That is, apart from William and Mat, who were both quite jittery. Mat was managing to control his nerves a lot better, but poor William kept glancing over to where Fred was supposed to be.

'Dearest, would you be a darling and check on Freddie for me?' Mary Rose said, taking charge and addressing her husband. She could see Mat and William were desperate to move on, but convention tied them to the small group. 'I know it is tiresome, but he is so very young. Would you? Perhaps you could take Mr Archer too. He may have some last-minute advice for Freddie, I'd hate nerves to get the better of the boy.'

Mat Dawson and William Archer didn't need telling twice. They both nodded, took their leave and headed over to the large paddock. They were just in time to see Fred mount up and felt a simultaneous flash of pride at the look of focus on the young jockey's face. Both adults noted with satisfaction that the Maid of Trent looked good.

Mat turned to William and said in a quiet voice, which was just loud enough for Fred to hear: 'The ride looks absolutely perfect, your lad will have no problems. I'm glad I've put a hefty wager on her to win now. I think I'll be going home a bit richer today.'

Fred stayed looking ahead, but William spotted a slight colouring to his cheeks. He'd heard alright.

'Right son, you're ready to go,' William said, clearing his throat. 'Just remember all we've told you and you'll be just fine.'

Fred nodded, but did not take his eyes off the horizon. Although he was listening to his father, he also had his own race strategy going over and over in his mind. He had to win this time. He just had to.

A few minutes later William and Mr Dawson made their way back to their families. They were still together in a large group and had moved, en masse, closer to the finishing line. Molly, who was there with her new husband Bert, had opened up a large hamper and was handing around small delicacies. The youngsters were especially appreciative.

The group collectively caught their breath when Fred and his competitors headed towards the start-line.

'I can't watch,' gasped Emma, closing her eyes.

'He'll be fine,' whispered Mary Rose. 'You know he is happiest when he is up on a horse. Come on, hold my hand. You'll help me with my nerves too.'

Emma gratefully took hold of Mary Rose's small hand and stared down the course.

'Come on Freddie,' she whispered.

The rest of her crowd, with the exception of Mary Rose, were nowhere near as restrained. They were all shouting and waving before the starter's flag went up. The air positively fizzed with excitement. Then, just when everyone felt they could no longer bear the anticipation, the riders were off.

The noise was tremendous. The crowd strained their eyes to see what was going on in the mass of brightly coloured silks and blur of chestnut, black and bay horses thundering towards them.

'I can see him!' shouted William. 'He's right in the middle of the bunch.'

'Good positioning,' confirmed Mat Dawson, with a nod.

'He's edging forward,' said Bert, somewhat breathlessly. 'Look, he was definitely the first over that jump.'

'He looks so small, compared to the others,' said Molly, her voice slightly muffled by the hand in front of her mouth. She looked like she may scream out in shock and distress at any moment. She was always very protective of young Freddie.

'Two jumps left, my son, you've got it, you've got it,' chanted William, his hands balled into fists. 'Show her the whip…'

Emma noticed her son was more than 'showing' the Maid of Trent the whip. He was whipping her very hard indeed. She winced, but then checked herself. It was not for her to judge.

'Let her run,' shouted Mat. 'Don't let up till you've passed the post.'

And then it was over. Fred sailed past the finishing post a clear length and a half in front of the next rider, Valley Boy. The noise of clapping and cheering was deafening. The Archers and Dawsons jumped around in joy, hugging each other and slapping each other on the back.

'What an amazing win,' Mat said to William, pumping his hand up and down in a firm handshake. 'That boy has some talent.'

'I told you, I told you,' grinned William Archer, who was rendered almost speechless by his son's triumph.

At that moment, Fred passed close by on his way to the winner's enclosure and the cheer that went up was deafening. Fred smiled back shyly. He was proud of what he had done, but while he prepared meticulously for every yard of the race, he had no idea how to deal with all the praise and adoration. It all felt a little bit too much for the young lad.

'We'll see you at the winner's enclosure!' yelled William, pronouncing 'winner' with loud relish.

Fred nodded and rode on. He was consumed by a complete and total feeling of joy. He had done it.

The crowds gathered around him as soon as he

entered the winner's enclosure. He barely managed to give his ride a pat before everyone seemed to be talking at him at once. He did his best to answer everyone, but it wasn't easy, particularly since he was still breathing hard from the race.

'Well done young Archer,' Mrs Wilan said, grabbing the Maid of Trent's reins in a proprietorial way. 'That was a very good race. How did she go for you?'

'Just as you said, madam. Steady until the last two jumps then she seemed to find another speed,' Fred smiled at his patron. 'I thought she could have kept going.'

'It was a good race, son,' interrupted William, before Mrs Wilan had a chance to properly respond. 'I'm sure that felt better than the Newmarket race, hey?'

'Yes Father, very much so and it is so lovely to see you're all here. Everyone has made it; Mother, Molly, my dear sisters and little brother. I bet he shouted the loudest, eh Bert?'

'Yes, that's true enough, young Fred. Especially when you went past that post. Oh, you did look grand.'

Freddie greeted each member of his family warmly. He hadn't seen them since Molly and Bert's wedding and missed them all terribly. Then, out of the corner of his eye, he caught the Dawsons, who were clearly holding back, giving him some space to be with his loved ones.

Fred quickly went over to them.

'Hello sir, and Mrs Dawson.' He smiled at Mat and Mary Rose and then touched his cap to Mat's brother and wife.

'Well done, Freddie, I couldn't have asked for anything better,' said Mat. 'You did us all proud.'

'That was a very good ride, lad,' John Dawson agreed. 'We were all glad to see your first win. May there be many more in the future, as we are sure there will be.'

Both Mr Dawsons carried on talking, but Fred was only half listening now. He was looking at Helen Dawson, who had squeezed between her father John and mother Grace. Fred had briefly met her before, but had never been close enough to talk. She was quite petite with large, almond-shaped eyes and a crown of glossy, yet utterly unruly, fair hair. Helen had an intriguing delicate, almost aristocratic look, quite similar to his mother's and looked far older than her ten years. Yet, it was her smile which Fred particularly liked though. It was one of those impish smiles you just can't help returning. He was convinced it would light up the most gloomy day.

'Well done Freddie,' she said confidently. 'You must be very happy. I really enjoyed watching the race. Were you nervous?'

'Thank you, Miss Dawson,' Fred said, doing his best to fight the colour that was rising to his cheeks. 'Yes I am pleased and, yes, I was a little nervous just before the start. Then, when the starter signalled, it just went. All I could see were the jumps and then the winning post. There was no time for anything else. I just had to win.'

Helen beamed one of her wonderful smiles and a sudden thought hit Freddie as he smiled back. He'd always thought there was no better feeling in the world than winning. It turns out, there may be something if not better, at least as good; a smile from a beautiful girl. Either way, he had had the most incredible day, perhaps the best in his whole life.

CHAPTER FOUR

The win at Newmarket was, as Mat Dawson predicted and William had hoped, the signal of the start of something big. Success didn't come easy though, and it didn't come fast. In 1871, still aged just fourteen, Fred had twenty-seven rides, but just three were winners. However, very often, it is those you do win that make all the difference.

For Fred, another real turning point was being asked to ride a colt called Salvanos in the Newmarket October Handicap of October 1871. Salvanos was a big, strong, wilful horse owned by Joe Radcliffe, who was better known to his friends as 'Holy Joe', for his rather unfortunate habit of blaspheming loudly during the excitement of watching his horses race. Holy Joe used to bet quite heavily, so it is perhaps little wonder he got carried away. In Salvanos' last race, the horse had bolted, leaving his rider helpless to do anything about it and Holy Joe had lost all his cash thanks to his lavish bets. Keen not to let history repeat itself, he asked Mat Dawson if he could recommend a lightweight jockey who was good with difficult horses.

'You'll want young Fred Archer,' Mat said, without hesitation. 'He's young, but I have never seen anyone handle a horse like it.'

On that recommendation, Holy Joe didn't argue. Fred was immediately engaged to ride Salvanos.

Mat Dawson was careful to fully brief Fred ahead of the race, but left the lad to work out his own strategy after that. Fred had enough experience by now and his master knew it was best to leave him to work things out for himself. Mat didn't mention the hefty bet Holy Joe had riding on his mount in the forthcoming race. He saw no need to pile on the pressure. Besides, the stakes were getting higher for each race Fred ran.

On the day of the race itself, Mat was pleased to see his protégé was as calm and composed as ever, even though Salvanos was already displaying signs of his wilfulness. From almost the moment the race began, the colt made a determined effort to run out, but Fred would not let him bolt. He kept him under control and the pair hit the lead almost immediately. No one really ever had a chance to challenge them after that and Salvanos finished comfortably ahead, much to the delight of Holy Joe and, of course, Fred who was as intent on winning as ever. Mat Dawson was particularly gratified to read a later write-up of the race which praised 'little Archer' for his 'coolness and steadiness', saying he rode like a veteran, despite his tender years.

Again, it was not all plain sailing after that. Indeed, in a subsequent race on Salvanos, this time in Cambridgeshire, the previously victorious pairing came an unseemly last. Poor old Holy Joe lost all the money he had won on the previous outing. Such is the excitement and lottery of the racetrack.

As time went on, the gap between winning and losing gradually closed. Fred was clearly realising the potential that so many people had seen in him from an early age. Although still painfully young, he was the figure in the stables all the lads looked up to now. Everyone wanted to be Fred Archer. Very often, he would walk into the yard and the entire area would go quiet. This was quite a feat because a busy yard is a noisy, frenetic place. It was simply that everyone stopped to stare at the talented young man, wondering what magic he had in his fingertips and toes that made horses run so fast for him.

His reputation was growing outside Heath House too. Fred didn't just do his job and forget about it. He'd remember every nuance of each horse he rode and would watch others he hadn't ridden just as keenly, studying the running and going over in his own head how he would win on that horse if he were ever asked to ride it. He'd read and re-read form and soon had an almost encyclopaedic knowledge of the major horses of the day, often considerably more so than the punters who would put a large amount of money on them.

Despite his tender years, Fred was also highly articulate and confident when it came to speaking about horses. Owners and trainers would often seek out his advice and were frequently struck by his perceptiveness. After each ride, Fred made a habit of telling the owners he rode for exactly how their horses had gone at various points in the race. He also had an uncanny knack of knowing how his rivals had fared, even if they were not even remotely closely placed during the running. It was as if he knew everything that was going on around him.

Mat Dawson could not have asked for anything more.

When Fred came out of his indentures, aged sixteen, Mat presented him with a watch inscribed: *For good conduct – Mathew Dawson.* Fred was bowled over by the gift.

'Thank you so much, sir. I will treasure this all my life,' Fred said, staring at the watch.

Mat nodded. He knew this young man was sincere. He meant the inscription too. Fred's behaviour was exemplary.

'You deserve it,' he said, patting him on the back. 'Your behaviour and dedication have been far above what anyone could expect.'

He paused, wanting to be sure Fred was going to take in the importance of what he wanted to say next.

'There is something else too.'

'Yes sir?'

'I'd like to make you the official lightweight jockey for Heath House.'

'Sir?'

'Yes, I know that's Fred Webb's position, but I would like you to take over. Fred seems to be having a great deal of difficulty in getting to grips with his weight. You seem to be pretty much on top of things, so it makes sense to change things around a bit. Are you all right with that?'

'Yes sir.' Fred nodded, his eyes wide with surprise. 'I am very honoured and won't let you down.'

'I know you won't.'

If Mat had looked carefully, he might have seen a trace of concern flash through those deep brown eyes of Fred's. While he was determined not to let Mat down and would train longer and harder than any lad in Heath House, Fred's weight was a constant concern.

Fred was, by now, 5 feet 7 inches, which was tall for a jockey. It also meant he was correspondingly heavier, which in turn meant the demands for him to keep his weight down were particularly onerous. His biggest fear was it wouldn't be long before Mat Dawson would be having a similar conversation with another lightweight, complaining about *Fred Archer's* inability to keep his weight down.

Fred had already seen his close friends Sam and Joe succumb to their 'weight problems'. Neither of them could keep their weight down to the punishing levels required for a jockey. Luckily Sam was happier exercising horses and looking after the yard, while Joe had proved invaluable in helping Mr Dawson in the office, working out weights, feeds, and travel routes, so they were both still gainfully employed at Heath House. But how much longer could Fred do the same, he wondered?

Fred's natural size meant he couldn't simply 'watch his weight' and achieve the level he needed by cutting down on large meals. If he wanted to remain 'lightweight' he had to actively lose weight. All the time. His diet had become a constant obsession. In his mind, it carried equal status with the training and preparation of the horses and took up a similar amount of time. Each day, Fred would spend lengthy periods in Turkish baths, which would force him to sweat for hours at a time. Most days he would barely eat a thing, just a tablespoon of hot caster oil for breakfast and half an orange, and a sardine and small glass of champagne for lunch, then nothing more. Hardly surprisingly the diet left him light-headed, irritable and low in energy, hardly adequate preparations for the physical exertions he had to endure with his strict training schedule.

In the run-up to race days, he switched to eating only his 'special mash', the somewhat ironic equine nickname he gave to the revolting mixture which gave him almost constant stomach cramps and confined him to the toilet for long, agonising periods each day. The special mash was a secret recipe perfected by the Dawson family, which consisted mainly of ingredients with a hugely laxative effect, such as grape juice, bran, and prunes, mixed with raw apple cider vinegar. It tasted, and smelt, as bad as it sounds and no attempt was ever made to make it even vaguely palatable. Mary Rose used to make a great vat of it and it was kept on a shelf in the pantry in the Dawson's kitchen. Jockeys used to come for their 'ration' if they had a race coming up and they needed to shed a few pounds. Most simply endured it for a few days, often cheating by adding a few spoons of sugar, or honey, to take away the foul taste. Fred would take it religiously an entire fortnight before a race, even more if he was really concerned about where he was tipping the scales. He refused to cheat with sweeteners too, even though he winced at each mouthful. He knew just how effective it could be. A fortnight of special mash and a stone and a half in weight would drop off his already painfully slim frame.

Although everyone was keen to spend time with him, particularly as he became more successful, Fred felt constantly lonely. Sam and Joe were still trusted confidants, but the long hours spent fasting, steaming, and in the toilet, made the young jockey feel isolated and excluded. He'd often glance at the other lads larking about in the yard and long to feel that carefree. Yet, at the same time, he knew exactly why he was doing what he was doing. He wanted to win and this was the only way.

Fortunately, there was some respite for Fred from a most unexpected source. During Fred's first race in Newmarket and subsequent celebrations, Molly and Bert had struck up a conversation with John and Grace Dawson and they all got on very well. Not long after, Molly and Bert were invited to go and work for the Dawsons; Molly in the house helping Grace and her children and Bert out on the farm and stables with John. With three girls and a son, the house was always busy and John had a large yard too. Grace would also entertain a great deal. The job came with a tied cottage, a tiny chocolate box, one-bedroomed, thatched dwelling, which was perfect for the newlyweds. Emma was sorry to see her young charge go, but always knew Molly would have to move on eventually. She was also delighted she would be living close to her Freddie. At least someone from the family would be nearby to keep an eye on him. It went a long way to assuaging her fears.

Fred was soon a frequent visitor, in fact he loved

going to Molly and Bert's little house, which was only a short walk from Heath House, and would pop over there whenever he was able. It felt like a little bit of home and Molly always made such a fuss of him. While she could see how painfully thin he was, she never said anything. She simply made sure he had a nice warm place to sit by the fire and talked to him of home.

'Do you remember that time that William Junior and you tried to have that running race at harvest time?' she'd reminisce. 'You ran straight into the path of that horse and cart which was going at such a lick. All the men were cheering, in their cups of cider, and all the ladies were screaming and wailing fit to burst they were so scared you were both going to be crushed. You fair copped it from your dad that time. I don't think I've ever seen your ma so cross either.'

Fred grinned. He remembered that episode very well. His father had tanned their hides and they'd been locked in their room for a week. Molly had sneaked in cakes and treats whenever she could and whispered stories about what else the village children were up to. Harvest was always such a wonderful time. All routines went out of the window as the community worked to get the crops in before the winter set in. The kids certainly took advantage of the more lax regime, with the menfolk working late nights and imbibing rather more cider and ale than usual to 'relax'.

Fred loved hearing Molly's stories, even though he had heard many of the same ones time and again. They were like food and water to him.

There was something else he really enjoyed about

his visits too. John and Grace's daughter, Helen, was a frequent presence and becoming ever more so. To begin with, Fred felt shy and awkward around her but, with some encouragement from Molly, he slowly became more forthcoming. Now, almost the moment he arrived at the cottage, he'd be looking about him to see if Helen 'just happened' to be walking by.

'She's a pretty one,' murmured Molly, catching him staring at her through the window one particular day. 'She's quite the young lady now.'

'Yes, I agree Molly,' Fred said, never once taking his eyes off Helen. 'I've always thought she is so pretty, but of course, Molly, not as pretty as you!'

'Oh, you're a charmer, I'll give you that,' laughed Molly. 'I always said it. You'd charm the birds from the trees.'

Fred was already on his feet. He gave Molly a hug as he got up to go to the door.

'Go on then, before you miss her,' Molly chided, giving him a quick kiss on the cheek.

Fred dashed outside to intercept Helen, just as she passed the front gate.

'Good afternoon, Helen,' he said, catching up with her. 'How are you today?'

Helen slowed her step and gave Fred a warm smile.

'I am well, thank you Fred, and yourself? How are the race preparations going? I saw you out on the course practising earlier.'

'You did?' said Fred, the colour rising to his face. He had had a strange feeling he was being watched. 'I think it is going all right. I'm not sure really. I prepare and prepare, but never quite feel I have done enough.'

Helen frowned. Fred was so highly thought of wherever he went, yet seemed to be the last person to recognise his own abilities.

'You push yourself too hard,' she said quietly, wary of stepping into a space where she was not supposed to go. She swallowed hard. She'd started now and couldn't stop. 'I know it is not my place to say, but since we know one another better now, I feel I must. I've seen you in the run-up to a race and you look exhausted. More and more so each time. If you don't mind me saying, you look especially weary today. It's hard work being a jockey, God knows I have heard it said a thousand times around these parts, but you seem to put so much more in than anyone else.'

Helen stopped abruptly. Fred was staring at her, open mouthed. She had gone too far, she knew it. She could have kicked herself. She should have stuck to conversations about the weather and the flora and fauna. These are the things nicely brought up young ladies are supposed to say. Things would have been fine then. The trouble was, while she was well brought up, she was never afraid to speak her mind and, to be fair, her mother and father encouraged her to have an opinion on all topics, especially horses. Perhaps also, since she had two sisters and one brother, she was used to fighting her corner. Either way, young Helen had been raised to hold her own. Most of the time though, she was careful to follow the norms of society, but if she felt comfortable, she was quick to speak her mind. She'd spent a lot of time with Fred now and the two of them had been getting along so well it just seemed the right time to say something. At least it did when she had started speaking. Seeing his apparently dumbfounded reaction, Helen began to wonder.

'I'm sorry,' she stammered. It was her turn to blush. 'I don't know what came over me.'

The silence between them seemed to stretch into eternity. Helen, who had averted her eyes downwards after her outburst, hardly dared to look up. She could hear them both breathing and wondered if her companion could hear the sound of her heart which seemed to be hammering at her chest. Finally she looked up. Fred was still staring at her with his bewitching dark brown eyes.

'You are right,' he said, his voice low. 'To speak frankly, as you have just been kind enough to do with me, I do feel I push myself hard. Probably much harder than I ought to. I just don't know any other way. It's been like this ever since I could remember. I just don't want to let anyone down. Not my father, or Mr Dawson, or all the people who believe in me. I suppose too, if I am honest, I make myself do it because I hate to lose. Always have done.'

He stopped talking. He was still staring at Helen and she returned his gaze without hesitation or shyness. Neither of them felt self-conscious.

'I didn't mean to be so forward,' Helen began. 'I just...'

'No, you were right to say something,' Fred interrupted. 'And I am glad it was you. It is nice to,' he paused, as if trying to summon up the courage to say something, 'have someone special to talk to.'

Helen caught her breath.

'And, am I? Someone special?'

Fred leaned forward and tenderly brushed a stray tendril of Helen's fair hair from her eyes.

'I think you know the answer to that, Helen Dawson.'

Helen smiled one of her most melting smiles and Fred beamed right back.

'Gosh, I didn't expect this when I wandered past this morning,' Helen breathed.

'Well, it has only taken me four years to summon up the courage to say it,' said Fred, laughing softly. 'I'm glad I finally have.'

'Me too.'

'Should we walk now? I am conscious we are standing very close to Molly and Bert's cottage and if I know Molly as I do, I suspect she's been watching us this whole time. It's not that she likes to spy, but I know she just won't be able to resist checking up on me.'

Helen glanced over her shoulder, her eyes wide.

'I think you may be right. Please give me your arm, Freddie.'

Helen hooked her arm through Fred's and the pair set off. Fred and Helen both grinned as they heard Molly calling for Bert in the background.

'Bert, Bert, you've got to come here, you'll never believe…'

'That'll give everyone something new to talk about,

won't it? I mean other than your triumphs on the racetrack.'

Fred giggled and the pair walked on.

After that, Helen and Fred were officially a couple, although to all intents and purposes the two of them had been destined for one another since the moment they first met.

Fred seemed to change completely after that too. While he was still exhausted by the harsh regime, he seemed happier and more certain of himself. It was as though a piece of a puzzle that had long been missing had now been found. With this happiness came a renewed confidence. Rather than simply answering the frequent enquiries of owners and trainers, who would often approach him for advice, Fred now began to actively seek them out. If he saw a horse he liked in a race, he would make a point of going up to an owner later in the day, congratulating them and then asking for an opportunity to ride their horse at a later date. With Fred's reputation now secure, most owners were flattered and only too delighted to let this up-and-coming young jockey have their patronage. Such requests did not happen often and when they did, they'd have been a fool not to accept them.

That year, Fred won the Great Lancashire Handicap on Lord Falmouth's Kingscraft, having clocked up an astonishing four hundred and twenty-two rides. Fred developed rivalries with the other promising young riders of the day, George Fordham and Henry Constable, and was devastated when Constable pipped him to the post to win the jockey's championship.

The following year, Fred corrected this, comfortably winning the championship with 147 wins to his name. It came at a price though. Fred had a final growth spurt, bringing him to 5 foot 8½ inches and keeping his weight under six stone became an agonising obsession. While he would never admit it, the constant wasting was beginning to affect his performance on the racetrack. On more than one occasion, he found his strength failing in the final few moments of a race. He had a personal dread that one day he would simply pass out and fall from his mount into certain calamity.

He kept his fears to himself though and did his best to keep them from Helen, although he always sensed she knew. In truth, she did. However, she knew equally well that Fred would never give up racing and, if he was racing, he had to win. Fred would have it no other way. If that was the case, and it was, he had little choice but to do what was required to keep ahead. All she could do was to support him and make sure he took as good care of himself as possible in the circumstances.

It became Helen's private mission to keep Fred upbeat and happy. She fed him with her love and affection, making sure he spent at least some time away from the track and stables each day. She partly took over Mary Rose's role of making sure Fred kept in constant touch with his family. Helen particularly liked Emma, who she had now met many times at race days and understood the close bond between mother and son. She found William Archer a little more difficult to get on with, but equally understood how much Fred sought out his father's approval.

At Helen's encouragement, Fred had bought his parents a hotel. It was, to him, the perfect way to solve their on-going money worries and ensure a decent income for the future. He had paid for the Andoversford Hotel with some of the winnings from the last few years. The large, Bath-stone hotel was just a few miles from Cheltenham racecourse and Fred loved going there to stay whenever he could.

The need for regular rest and respite was growing greater each passing year. Fred was now a favourite of a number of prominent owners, most notably Lord Falmouth and much in demand elsewhere. His list of fans seemed to be growing almost daily. It was about this time that the redoubtable Duchess of Montrose first began to cast an interested eye over the young jockey. The Duchess had a reputation as a formidable woman on the racing circuit. She once upbraided her vicar for praying for fine weather because, as she pointed out, he should know very well her horse was running the next day and preferred the going deep!

Anyone who had been at the end of one of the Duchess' tongue lashings knew very well her voice could carry and the things she said would cut deep. In another example of her outspokenness, she once loudly accused Major Egerton, the handicapper at Newmarket, of treating her unfairly.

'I presume, Major Egerton, from the way you handicap my horses, you are anxious to ride them yourself,' legend had it that she declared haughtily. 'I can only say your ambition will not be gratified.'

Mat Dawson was not surprised when the Duchess sought him out after another one of Fred's triumphs. It was well-known that, despite her advancing years, she had somewhat of a weakness for handsome young men.

'Freddie, I'd like to introduce you to the Duchess of Montrose,' he said, calling him over in the winner's enclosure.

Fred took the Duchess' offered hand and bowed, as he knew he had to do. 'Madam,' he said.

'I saw your ride,' she said, her voice loud and confident. 'I was impressed.'

'That is very kind of you. You had a horse in that race also, did you not?'

'Macheath. He was unplaced, which was most disappointing.'

Fred nodded.

'He started well, but seemed to run out of steam about halfway,' Fred said, once again demonstrating his broad understanding of each race he ran. 'I've seen him run better. He looks a bit heavy on the shoulder.'

'Interesting,' the Duchess murmured, looking Fred up and down. 'You seem very confident for such a young man.'

'Thank you madam. I just say what I see.'

'Well, I shall be keeping a close eye on you from now on,' smiled the Duchess, reverting to her louder, more commanding voice.

'Thank you madam,' Fred repeated, realising he was being dismissed.

Mat gave Fred a barely discernible wink as he left to rejoin his group. It seemed Heath House was about to gain itself another rich patron, although the Duchess of Montrose would be no easy person to work with. She was well-known to change her trainers almost as often as she changed her mind. However, if any jockey would retain her interest, it would be Fred. Of that, Mat Dawson could be sure.

CHAPTER FIVE

Each season, Fred's toll of winners mounted steadily and with them he received more offers of rides. Many of the biggest names in racing of the day wanted Fred and he was happy to oblige. By this time the young jockey had gained a reputation for betting heavily on his own races, but he always put his owners' interests first and everyone knew that. While some people whispered about the greed and impetuousness of a newly successful young man, few were openly critical. What was most remarkable was that no one really stopped to consider how out of character this high stakes gambling was for Fred.

Younger jockeys knew how kind and generous Fred could be. In fact, truth be told, he was a bit of a soft touch for anyone with a hard luck tale. He'd give up his last penny to help a fellow jockey in trouble. The real story behind his supposedly grasping nature was the constant demands being made on him at home. William Archer had always been careless with money, but now Fred had become successful, he openly lived off his famous son. William lived the life of the well-to-do men he bought and sold horses for, using Fred's name to secure credit for himself and the family with wild abandon. It was invariably down to Fred to meet the demands of creditors and with each week that passed, the sums seemed to grow. Whenever the clamour to settle debts grew too loud, William would simply pass a handful of chits to Fred, mumbling something about 'needing a bit of help here, son'.

Emma knew something was wrong, but while the day-to-day running of the hotel was largely left in her hands, she was never completely aware of the finances. Her husband carefully hid his largest excesses and Fred was not about to worry his beloved mother with such vulgar details. If she asked Fred about it, on one of her son's frequent visits, he'd assure her everything was fine.

'But I'm just not sure how we are paying for all of these things,' she'd say helplessly.

Fred would make up a story about a grateful patron tipping his father a large sum to clear a debt, or some other such excuse.

'I don't want you paying for everything,' she insisted suspecting, quite rightly, that Fred had more of a hand in things than he was letting on. 'You've earned that money. I want you to think about making a home for yourself. That will cost money.'

Luckily for Fred, he was getting some good advice about his finances. He had a growing friendship with Lord Falmouth, built on a mutual respect between the pair. Fred was now on a retainer with Lord Falmouth and invariably performed admirably on his horses.

However, their relationship was based on more than just a good working partnership. Lord Falmouth liked and respected the young jockey. He enjoyed his quick and ready wit and loved hearing his frank assessments of races. So many riders simply did their job and counted their winnings. Fred, on the other hand, would give a yard-by-yard account of every race. For a horse owner, this sort of information wasn't just interesting to hear, it was gold dust. Lord Falmouth returned the favour by becoming Fred's confidant and advisor, particularly on financial matters. In fact, Fred became a frequent guest at his benefactor's palatial home.

Although it was difficult for Fred, because of demands elsewhere, he readily and gratefully accepted Lord Falmouth's advice on putting away at least some of the large sums he was earning and making some shrewd investments. One of those investments he made was to buy land on the outskirts of Newmarket.

'A wise investment, young man,' Lord Falmouth concurred, when Fred told him that he had followed his advice.

Fred was spending another weekend at Lord Falmouth's large home, as he did more and more these days. The pair enjoyed each other's company and Fred was a huge attraction at the Lord's soirees and dinner parties. Everyone wanted to be near this young, talented jockey. On this particular weekend though, nothing was planned and the two men simply relaxed and enjoyed each other's company.

'I'm thinking of building a house,' Fred said.

Lord Falmouth noticed the jockey seemed a little

nervous and unsure of himself. It was like he wanted to say something, but didn't know how.

'Oh yes,' he said, nonchalantly.

Lord Falmouth knew Fred well enough by now to know it was always best to leave him to tackle things in his own time. He was a very bright lad, but had a habit of being very deliberate in his speech. Fred was a stickler for planning things out and getting things exactly right. It was reflected in everything he did, from his riding to how he framed things he said.

'I would like to call my new house Falmouth.'

A huge grin swept across the older man's face.

'I hardly know what to say…'

'…You've been so good to me,' interrupted Fred. 'Your patronage has meant everything and I always seem to be here cluttering up your house.'

'Not at all. It is I who should be grateful to you. You have transformed my stables and for that I should be forever thankful. I am flattered and honoured that you would use my name.'

It was typical of Fred to be unassuming and humble. It was reflected in everything he did. Despite his huge success, he was still living in Spartan quarters at Heath House, six years after he had first begun there. Although, by now, he had graduated out of the dorms used by stable lads, he still only had one small, sparsely furnished room, ornamented with racing pictures and trophies. Although Mat and Mary Rose were hugely fond of him, Fred had no special treatment. The interesting thing is, Fred didn't feel he deserved special treatment either. This was despite notching up literally hundreds of winners each year, which had garnered him a huge following. Crowds would turn up to watch if they knew Fred Archer was in the running, yet he hardly seemed to notice.

After securing Lord Falmouth's approval, Fred returned to more comfortable ground and began to talk animatedly about a forthcoming race. Indeed, the house was almost all but forgotten when the pair got into a lively discussion about George Fordham who had missed most of the 1877 season. It appeared that Fred's arch rival was succumbing to alcoholism and was apparently drinking large quantities of gin each day. Neither Lord Falmouth nor Fred could quite believe how his life had spiralled out of control so quickly.

'He seemed fine last time we were up against one another.' Fred shook his head. 'Mind you, that was last season. He was as tough an opponent as ever. I knew he liked a drink or two, but it's totally changed him. I guess the dieting can't help.'

'You keep yourself healthy,' warned Lord Falmouth, only half-jokingly. 'It is all very well this starving yourself all the time, and I know you have to do it, but try to keep everything else on an even keel.'

'Helen helps me do that, sir,' Fred said, his dark eyes lighting up at the mention of her name.

'Indeed she does,' his friend agreed. 'You make a handsome couple.' After spending time at Lord Falmouth's home, Fred decided to visit his parents on his way home. He'd not seen them for a while, thanks to his racing commitments, and missed them greatly. He missed his dear brothers and sisters too, especially

Emily. He arrived early on Saturday morning, having not sent word he would be there for the weekend. He wanted it to be a complete surprise. The moment he arrived though, something felt wrong. He couldn't put his finger on it, but the hotel which normally felt so lively and cheerful, seemed to be shrouded in an atmosphere of gloom.

'Is my mother here?' he asked Dolly, the housekeeper who greeted him at the front door.

'She is, sir,' Dolly said, giving Fred a little bob of a curtsy. The young woman was plainly in awe of the famous jockey and hadn't quite worked out in her mind the best way to treat him. 'She is in the drawing room. Can I take your hat?'

'Thank you Dolly. And my father?'

'He's in Cheltenham with your brother William Junior,' the young lady replied, looking a little nervous now.

Fred frowned. His mother had said William Junior was racing that day, but had told him his father would not be going along too. It was no point taking out his irritation on the staff. She wasn't to know.

'Thank you,' he said again. 'I'll show myself through.'

Fred strode down the corridor towards the drawing room, his footsteps echoing against the richly coloured oak floorboards. He reached the large doorway and as he gripped the brass latch he couldn't escape the strangest feeling of foreboding.

'Mother,' he said as he stepped confidently into the room, doing his best to shake off the odd sensation.

'Freddie!' she cried, leaping to her feet, her sewing falling to the floor, scattered and forgotten in her pleasure.

She hurried forward and hugged Fred.

'Let me look at you,' she said, stepping back, her hands still planted firmly on her son's arms. 'You look so well, but a little pale perhaps. Are you getting enough food?'

Fred laughed despite himself.

'We have this same conversation every time. The answer is a resounding no, but I am not able to get enough food because I can't, so there you are. You will have to find something else to get worried about. This situation is not going to change any time soon.

'Now, more importantly, where is everyone? You said my father would be here.'

Emma nodded and sighed. She indicated with her hand her son had better sit down.

'Let me get us some tea first. You have had a long train ride.'

Fred sat down in the deep armchair which was on one side of the fire place. Once his mother got back from organising tea with Dolly she settled into the chair opposite, after first picking up her sewing and bundling it somewhat unceremoniously into a large wicker basket.

Emma smiled at her son. Whatever happened in their lives, this boy was a source of such great pride for her.

'William really wanted to be here today, but he had to make a last-minute change of plan. We had a bit of a strange day yesterday and your brother was very upset. Your father thought it best to accompany him to the race in Cheltenham.'

Fred shifted in his chair, wondering what the strange event could possibly be. His older brother was not easily spooked. None of the Archer brothers had ever needed their hands held before. William Senior had personally seen to it that they had been very hardy from a young age. Tears were seen as a weakness the Archer boys could well do without.

Emma was a bit more circumspect. She knew very well that while her boys rarely vented their true emotions in front of her husband, they were all very sensitive. William Junior had always seemed especially so and particularly hated to hear about the death of a fellow jockey. It would change his whole demeanour when he heard about an accident.

'What happened?' said Fred gently.

Emma smoothed down her skirt. She looked unusually anxious.

'You remember Father Charles Wood?' she began.

'Remember?' asked Fred. 'Of course, you introduced me last time I was here, after the service. Why?'

'I hardly know where to begin. I was here yesterday getting things ready for your visit and I heard the most terrible commotion outside. There was a lot of shouting and screaming. Your brother came rushing in and said there had been the most dreadful accident. I'm still not quite sure what happened, but somehow the Father came off his horse right outside the hotel and fell into a pile of wooden posts.'

Emma looked down. She was clearly very upset.

'That's awful,' Fred soothed. 'Did something spook the horse maybe? It can happen very easily, for the strangest things. I remember once at Heath House…'

Fred stopped. His mother's expression was so lost and miserable.

'I'm sorry, please do go on. Was he hurt badly?'

'As soon as William Junior told me what had happened, I told Eddie at the desk to call for the doctor, but…'

Emma's voice faltered. Fred didn't interrupt.

'…But William Junior said he thought it was too late. He said there was so much blood. It was dreadful. He was shaking so badly. It really upset him.'

'I am so sorry Mother. How awful.'

Emma nodded.

'The doctor was here within ten minutes but there was nothing anyone could do for him. There were so many people here. Such a crowd. I just can't believe he is gone. I was so fond of him. We all were.'

Fred wasn't sure what to say. This sad story explained the gloomy atmosphere in the hotel. Emma had had all the blinds drawn as a mark of respect.

'Your brother took it very badly,' Emma went on, her words tumbling out in her sadness. 'He thought… I thought… we both thought it was a bad omen. I get these feelings, you know. I didn't want him to ride today and he felt the same. I said he mustn't go, but, but…'

Emma looked down and was breathing deeply. Fred knew she was trying not to cry but fighting a losing battle. She raised her hands to her face as though her fingertips could perhaps hold the tears in.

'You probably think me foolish. I worry though and I just get a feeling like the family is being punished.'

Fred frowned. This didn't make any sense. He couldn't imagine why his mother could feel this way. What on earth would they be punished for? They'd done nothing wrong.

'Don't be silly, Mother. None of us have done anything wrong. We've all lived good, honest, blameless lives. We work hard, go to church on Sundays and give what we can to those less fortunate. I can't imagine what you think we've done that deserves punishment. You must stop this foolish talk. You're clearly getting William Junior all in a flap with this nonsense.'

Fred didn't like being so harsh on his mother, but he didn't like seeing her this way either. Emma swallowed hard and nodded. She couldn't tell Fred about her innermost fears. She couldn't tell anyone why she feared divine retribution. Not now. Not ever.

'No, no, you are right,' she said straightening up. 'Your father said something very similar.'

Then she chuckled, despite herself.

'Although I might add, he didn't say it in your gentle way!'

Fred smiled.

'Well, I can imagine. When do you expect them home? Then we can all celebrate the latest Archer family triumph on the racecourse and put all this behind us. You are right to grieve for the Father, but don't think it is anything less than a shocking accident.'

Emma brightened. Everything always felt so much better when Freddie was around. He was probably right, she thought. How could she be so silly? It was just a sad, tragic accident.

'Where on earth is that tea?' she exclaimed, checking herself. 'I've been so busy talking I forgot all about it. Let me hurry things along and then you can tell me all about things at Heath House. I can't wait to hear how things are with Helen. I've been hearing all sorts from Molly, but I know how fanciful she can be.'

Emma leapt to her feet and Fred was pleased to see she seemed herself again.

'Goodness me, what is keeping that girl?' she said, hurrying towards the door.

Fred settled back in his chair and closed his eyes. He had never lived at the hotel, so couldn't truly call it 'home' but he always felt relaxed and safe there. He was surrounded by familiar furniture and trinkets and relished spending time with his loved ones. Even though he had come to love Heath House, there was a part of him that still felt he missed out on time with his family.

He must have nodded off, exhausted by the journey and the hard week's work beforehand. He was just a few days away from another big race, so he'd been on his special mash for a while now and his reserves of energy were low. Fred certainly didn't notice his mother return with the tray of tea. She paused at the door the moment she caught sight of her slumbering son and then slowly backed out. She understood how hard he worked and loved it that he could come back to her and feel relaxed enough to drop off.

Emma issued orders to the staff to keep out of the drawing room and asked that they were as quiet as possible at that side of the hotel. Then she went to the kitchen to oversee preparations for that evening's supper. It was a rare treat to get the whole family together and even though she knew Fred and his older brother would barely eat a thing, she was determined to make it a relaxed and convivial occasion.

Fred awoke in confusion a few hours later. The drawing room was almost in darkness and the fire had long since burned down. Just a few orange embers were left, casting a pathetic glow in the grey ashes. He felt stiff, uncomfortable and a little disorientated. For a few seconds he wondered where he was, struggling to work out the unfamiliar shadows in the room. He'd just realised he was in his parents' hotel when the true source of his confusion dawned upon him. There was a cacophony of shouts and crying in the corridor outside. It was such a change from the usual sounds in the hotel, which were the odd clatter of crockery, low voices, and distant thumps and bumps as things were moved around. These noises were more akin to a particularly tense race day, except there were no cheers accompanying the shouts. No, all he could hear were tears and wails.

Fred leapt to his feet and ran to the door. His heart was thumping and he felt dizzy from standing up so abruptly. Ignoring his own discomfort, he gripped the door latch and wrenched the door open. He raced out into the dimly lit corridor and headed in the direction of the commotion. He was almost too scared to know what he might find, but knew he had to get to whatever it was that was causing all the upset.

Suddenly, he pulled up short. His eyes were open wide and his hand flew to his mouth in horror. Nothing made sense. His mother was on the floor, her long dress ballooned out around her. Her head was in her hands and she was crying hysterically, deep rasping sobs that wrenched her entire body.

His father William, usually such a confident, upright man, full of bluff and swagger, was leaning back against the door jamb as though his legs were so weak they would no longer hold him up. He seemed diminished in height and was staring into the middle distance with wild, unfocussed eyes. Surrounding this extraordinary scene were dozens of people, some with familiar faces and some Fred had never seen before.

Fred walked slowly forward. Each step felt like agony because a great part of him didn't want to get any closer. He didn't want to ask the obvious question: what had happened? There was a part of him that already knew that whatever it was that had happened would change things forever.

As he got closer, he recognised a very familiar face: his good friend Joe from Heath House.

'Joe? Joe? What on earth are you doing here? What is going on?'

Joe looked distraught. He stepped forward and gripped Fred firmly by his shoulders.

'You need to prepare yourself, my friend,' he said

quietly and urgently. 'I have the most terrible news.'

Fred stared. None of this seemed to make sense. Part of him wondered if he was still actually asleep and this was some awful nightmare. He realised he was struggling to breathe.

'It's your brother, William Junior, there has been the most awful accident,' Joe said, still gripping Fred's shoulders. Joe felt his friend's knees begin to buckle and didn't relax his grip lest Fred dropped like a stone.

'How?' Fred whispered, his voice hoarse. 'Is he… alive?'

Joe looked down and shook his head slowly from side to side. He felt Fred lurch to the right as his legs finally gave way and it took all Joe's strength to stop him slumping to the floor.

Fred let out a howl of anguish.

'How?' he repeated, more quietly this time.

Joe swallowed hard. He didn't want to go on, but knew that he must.

'I was there for the races, talking to your father, I saw the whole thing,' he began slowly.

Fred stared at him intently, his bewitching brown eyes betraying just how hard he was finding it to grasp the enormity of the tragedy. Joe couldn't bear the look of agony on his friend's face.

'It was all going well with only three horses in the race,' Joe went on hesitantly, ready to stop at a moment's notice, if it all proved too much. 'It was the last fence and William Junior, well, he was second place. Salvanie was a nose ahead but just seem to stumble and young Will just fell.

'He just fell,' Joe repeated. 'His horse landed on him. He had no time to roll away. It all happened so fast.'

Joe glanced down at Emma, who was still slumped on the floor. She was quiet now, listening to the story intently. Inside she was praying for a different ending. Maybe if the story was told again, there could be a different one. It could happen. Couldn't it?

'We rushed over, your dad and me. We could see he was unconscious and we knew it looked bad, but we just hoped. Y'know, we've all seen this happen before. Sometimes a jockey is lucky and sometimes, well, sometimes they are not.'

The room was completely silent now. Everyone was staring at Joe.

'There was blood coming from his ear,' he said quietly. 'It looked bad. We didn't give up hope though. They came and took him to Captain Cotton's house. The doctor did everything he could, everything. There was no hope though. He never woke at all.'

Joe looked back down at his feet. He hated to do this. This sort of accident was every jockey's worst nightmare. Describing such a thing was bad enough, but for it to happen to a family friend was the worst possible outcome.

'I am so very sad for you and Mr and Mrs Archer,' Joe finished. 'I can't imagine what this might be like for you all.'

'Thank you, Joe,' Fred said quietly.

Fred was willing himself to recover. He wanted to collapse and cry and shout, but he knew he had to be strong. Stepping back, he bent low and gripped his mother's hand.

'Mother, please allow me,' he said gently.

Emma allowed herself to be helped to her feet. Her large brown eyes looked hollow and lifeless. Her expression was of pure shock and abject sadness.

'A parent should not live to see the death of their child, it is not right,' she breathed. 'Why didn't the Lord take me? It is me that should have gone.' She turned to face Fred. 'I told you,' she said, faltering. 'What happened yesterday was an omen. We're being punished.'

'Don't say that, Mother. I've already said, that doesn't make sense. It is two awful accidents. Just a coincidence. Nothing more.'

Turning to Dolly who was standing nearby, Fred called her over.

'Can you take the mistress to her room and see to it that she is comfortable. I will call the doctor and ask him to give her a tonic. She has had the most dreadful shock. Eddie? Can you take my father to the bar and fix him a stiff drink?'

Fred took charge, directing the large crowd, allotting each person a task. People seemed grateful to be given direction by the young man. It was somehow comforting to have a job to do, however incidental. It took their minds away from the pain of what had happened. For Fred too, coordinating the grieving crowd numbed his heart. His brother William Junior was gone.

Nothing would ever be the same again.

CHAPTER SIX

The next week passed in a blur for the Archer family. Fred, Charles, and the girls stayed close to their father and mother's side but the misery each of them felt as individuals created a gulf between them no one knew how to cross. The hotel was full of people coming to pay their respects and offering to help and support the family but of course they couldn't bring them the one thing they all really wanted: William Junior.

The funeral was well attended, with people coming from far and wide to show their loyalty to the well-known racing family. Again though, the Archers barely registered the outpouring of affection. Each was consumed by their personal misery. Fred felt like his heart might break when his mother broke down in tears as the simple wooden coffin was lowered into the soil.

After the service, the guests all made their way to the hotel and there were many familiar faces from the racing world among them. Now the ordeal of the burial was over, William and Emma were a little more conscious of the world around them and were amazed at how well loved their eldest son had been, yet still found it hard to interact in any meaningful way with the assembled throng. The family were, however, grateful that Molly stepped in, racing to be at their side as soon as she heard. The former housekeeper was wonderful, taking charge helping with the teas and food. Bert was, as ever, with Molly and stood by silently watching the whole sad business take place, helping out where he could.

It was late evening by the time everyone had left. Emma slumped into her chair beside the fireplace and stared vacantly into the embers. Fred joined her, settling into the chair opposite, unsure of what to say.

'I am so sad to see you this unhappy,' he began, his voice trailing off. He took a deep breath and tried again. 'Is there anything you would like, or anywhere you would like to go?'

Emma didn't answer. Fred wondered if she had heard. His mother seemed to be staring intently at the fire, her eyes wide.

'Mother?'

'Dear sweet Freddie,' she said with a start. 'I am sorry. Goodness, what would I do without you, Charles, and the girls? You must not worry about me. I will keep busy and that will help heal the sadness I feel. And you can help me by looking after yourself a bit better.'

The words left unsaid were, '*I can't bear to lose another son.*' They both knew it.

Fred cleared his throat. It seemed prudent to

change the conversation.

'I will call as often as I can and all you have to do is write if you need anything,' he said. 'I think I will go to stay with Lord James for a short while, he has been quite insistent that I go. It seems the best for us all. I do feel that if I go the crowds will stop hounding the hotel and give you and Father a little peace.'

Emma nodded. Neither of them had quite got used to Fred's growing fame. The young jockey handled it well most of the time, but in a situation like this it was certainly an added burden and one his mother absolutely did not need to be faced with right now. The press had virtually laid siege to the hotel once the news about Fred's brother broke. It would be far better for everyone if Fred moved on and let it be known he had done so too.

'I am glad you are going to stay with him,' Emma said. 'It will give you a rest too, my dearest. Maybe you will think about eating a little more? I do worry how thin you have become.'

'Maybe after the next race, Mother.'

Fred stood up to take his leave and Emma did the same, stepping forward and hugging her son tightly.

Fred left with a very heavy heart and took the train east to go and stay with Lord James. His thoughts instantly turned to his dear departed brother. The pair had always got on so well, far better in fact than with his younger sibling Charles, although they were all close. It was simply that he and William Junior had done so much riding together when they were young and by the time Fred left home at eleven, Charles had barely started racing. William Junior and Fred also thought alike and enjoyed the same group of friends. Fred could always confide in Will, knowing it would go no further. This had continued largely into adulthood, with Fred still confiding in his brother whenever they met. Now he was famous, it was difficult to find friends he truly trusted. It made sense to stick with the confidants of his youth. At least it had. Until now.

As the train steamed noisily through the lush countryside, Fred sat back, closed his eyes and travelled back in time. He pictured William Junior, together with him and Charles. The three of them were laughing, sharing a joke beside the river close by to their cottage. He remembered the scene he was picturing as though it was yesterday. His father, usually such a stickler for discipline, had ordered them all to get ready for training and then had been waylaid by something. He couldn't remember what now – possibly a large delivery of ale! Instead of dutifully getting on with their duties, the three brothers had wagged off and gone for a swim in the river. It was freezing cold and they were all very well aware they'd get a beating later, but right then they didn't care. They felt so free, so alive and so invigorated. He could see their younger selves splashing around, laughing and joking. Fred smiled to himself as he drifted off to sleep. *No one really ever dies*, he thought to himself, *not if you remember them like this.*

A few hours later, feeling infinitely more refreshed, Fred was settled into Lord James' beautiful drawing room. His companion searched his face to find traces of sadness and was pleased to see he was bearing up well.

'Oh Fred, I am so sorry for your loss. I know William Junior was a fine young man and he will be missed so by many folk. How are your mother and father?'

Lord James was sitting on a large leather sofa and Fred was standing by the mantelpiece, his back to the large picture-book window which looked out over the beautifully manicured grounds. When he had finished speaking the only other sound in the room was the imposing tick of the grandfather clock in the far corner.

'Yes, it is very sad indeed,' Fred agreed after a pause. While he was learning to bear his grief, he still had to gather all his strength to speak about his brother. 'I have not spent as much time as I'd like with Will over the past few years. As always with my family, spending time with one another seemed to have taken second place to all of our racing commitments. We had planned a hunting weekend together and were both looking forward to that, but it wasn't to be.

'It is kind of you to ask after my parents. I spent a few days with them both after the funeral. Dear Mother is so quiet and Father finds it hard to talk about it at all. It was him that told William Junior not to cancel the ride after our friend Mr Woods died just outside the hotel after a fall from his horse. Will had seen it happen and it upset him greatly. He said it was a bad omen. My mother felt the same.

'I don't blame my father, though. We would have all said the same to him, but Father has taken it especially bad. Time is, as they say, the only thing that will heal them now.'

The pair lapsed into silence. Lord James ached to do something to help his serious young friend, but knew there was little he could do. Just at that moment, the door swung open and three dogs bounded in, followed up by a very embarrassed-looking young lad.

'Sir, oh sir, I am so sorry,' faltered the boy. 'They got away from me.' Lord James laughed.

'You see Fred, my boy, they just sense you are here and are impatient to be taken across the fields when we go out for a ride.'

Fred smiled as he smoothed the coat of the large chocolate brown dog nearest to him, patting another with his other free hand. He was always at his most relaxed among four-legged creatures.

'Oh you three, calm down,' chided Lord James, his voice still friendly. 'Well, I can see we will get no peace until they are taken out. Come on, dear boy, let us go for a ride and see what bit of fresh air will do for our spirits.'

Fred was pleased to have an excuse to get outside. There was no use perpetually dwelling on his brother's death. It was just too distressing.

'That is a very good idea, sir, I would like that very much and it is such a warm day too. I hear you have two new horses in your yard. How are they? Are you pleased with them?'

The subject safely changed, the two fell into step and followed the lad out with the dogs. It was not that they didn't want to discuss the tragedy, simply that neither man saw the use of it. Although an unlikely pairing, they had always found comfort in each other's company. For Lord James, it was nice to feel closer somehow to Emma. For Fred it was exactly the distraction he needed.

The break at Lord James' also sealed a thought that had been growing in Fred's mind for some time: he would ask Helen to marry him. Life was short, he knew that now. It didn't make any sense to waste time. If there is a chance of happiness, one should grasp it with both hands.

He nervously broached the subject while out riding with Lord James. He valued his companion's opinion and was wondering if it was inappropriate to be thinking this way so soon.

'I... I... I was thinking of asking Mr Dawson if I could have Helen's hand,' Fred said slowly.

Lord James broke out into a warm smile. He turned in his saddle and held his hand out towards Fred.

'Well done,' he said, shaking him warmly by the hand. 'Well done. She really is quite charming.'

Fred blushed a little.

'Thank you. I'm just not sure if it is, well, too soon after… well, not the right time to ask.'

'It is absolutely the right time,' Lord James said. 'In fact, there could never be a better time. You deserve happiness and I know your parents will be thrilled. A good wedding is just what everyone needs to look forward to.'

Lord James noticed Fred had visibly relaxed a little now he had said what he'd wanted to say.

'You are very kind. Thank you. I think you are right. I just hope Helen agrees.'

'Oh, I don't think you will get any arguments there,' smiled Lord James, urging on his mount. 'She will be the happiest woman on Earth.'

After a few days with Lord James, Fred returned to Heath House and went straight to see John Dawson. John was not altogether shocked to see him looking so solemn and purposeful and immediately guessed the reason for his visit. He did his best to look surprised though.

'Thank you for taking the time to see me, sir,' Fred said, sounding unusually formal. Fred was a big favourite with John Dawson. Even if he had not liked him on his own account, which he did, he could hardly fail to be swayed by his brother Mat's constant glowing endorsements.

'As you know, I have been moderately successful on the racetrack and your bother, Mat, seems to think I have a sound future. I certainly intend to keep working hard and, God willing, I will continue to do well. I have the support of some rich patrons too, so my financial future is secure.' Fred cleared his throat.

'The reason I wanted to speak with you today was to ask if you would be willing to allow me the honour of marrying your daughter. I would like to ask for Helen's hand.'

John's face broke into a smile. Fred stared at him, his own expression still deadly serious, as though he dare not to smile back until he heard the reply.

'It would be our honour too,' John said, getting up and holding out his hand to shake the hand of his future son-in-law. 'We have long hoped for this moment and I know how happy this will make Helen.

I'll not stand in your way, Fred. In fact, I will welcome you into the family with a glad heart. I know my brother will be very pleased indeed to have the 'tin man' close to home.'

The 'tin man' was a nickname given to Fred a few years before. Mat had made a joking reference to Fred being 'that damned long-legged, tinscraping young devil' and the sobriquet had stuck.

Fred broke into a grin at last.

'That is wonderful news, really wonderful,' he stammered out, blushing and grinning at the same time.

For Fred, it was a dream come true. Helen had, for so long, been his confidant and his rock. The thought that they would spend the rest of their lives together was almost too much to imagine. Now all he had to do was speak to Helen.

As always, Fred took his time. He went through all the options and worked out his strategy. He always wanted every event he took part in to be perfect, but this one was just a little more special than all the rest.

He obviously got his planning just right too. Helen was thrilled when Fred formally proposed a day later. Fred surprised her on one of their daily walks, dropping to one knee in their favourite spot. It was a clearing close to the top of a hill above Heath House, where it was possible to see the entire farm and stables below. There was a large fallen oak there that must have lain there for years. In the centre was the perfect hollowed-out place for two people to sit and look out over the farm. In fact, so many young courting couples had sat there over the years whispering their endearments, it had been worn smooth.

Fred had led Helen to their usual spot, sat her down in 'their' place and then taken up his position. Helen gasped, because there could only be one reason for this, but she let her lover say the words anyhow. Her eyes filled with tears of happiness as Fred began to speak.

'I love you Helen,' he said. 'I always have. Will you marry me?'

'Yes,' sobbed Helen. 'Yes I will.'

She threw her arms around Fred's neck and sobbed even harder now.

'Hey, you are supposed to be happy,' Fred laughed. 'You're not going to the gallows.'

'I am happy, so very happy. I just can't believe it.'

Fred hugged her warmly. This, he knew, was all he had ever wanted. If everything was taken away from him now, the horses, the money, the rich patrons and the adulation, he wouldn't mind. Just as long as he had his Helen, everything in the world was all right.

Fred and Helen spent the rest of the day making plans. While they both couldn't wait to get married, Fred wanted to be sure they had a home to live in as newlyweds.

'There's not enough room in my quarters at the stables, although I could move my trophies off the cabinet and you could sleep there,' he joked.

'I don't care, I'd sleep in the straw with the horses if it meant we could be together,' Helen beamed.

'Be careful what you wish for,' Fred said. 'Mind

you, those horses live pretty well. I'll ask Mr Dawson if he has room for one more fine thoroughbred.'

Fred ducked as Helen threw a handful of grass at him, her face set in an indignant pout.

'No, don't worry my darling. The home I have in mind will be fit for a queen. Just you wait.'

Helen agreed to be patient and listened in rapt excitement as Fred prattled on about his plans for Falmouth.

'It sounds so grand,' she said.

'Nothing but the best for my love.'

The next task was to tell Emma and William Archer the news. Fred knew his mother would be thrilled. She had long loved Helen and had already dropped some fairly substantial hints that it was time her son thought about settling down. However, she was still in mourning over William Junior.

As it was, Emma was indeed delighted. In fact, she couldn't have been happier to hear the news, although Fred half-suspected she already knew. Emma had obviously been getting some fairly extensive reports from Molly, because every time Fred saw his mother she seemed to know a suspiciously large amount about the courtship. Nevertheless, the mood of the whole family lifted.

In the weeks that followed, Helen, Molly, Emma and Emily plunged into making wedding plans. Fred did his best to offer his help, but was, as always, swept up with riding commitments. Helen increasingly felt she had to insist that Fred took some time for himself and encouraged him to take long walks.

'Not all exercise needs to be on the back of a horse,' she joked, as they took one of their walks. 'You canter by so fast, I bet you never get to enjoy the beautiful countryside we live in.'

'Aye, you are right there,' he said, squeezing her hand as he stared out to the horizon.

'And, if you are good, I will tell you all about my wedding plans,' Helen trilled.

Fred smiled.

'You said it was all top secret,' he said. 'Does this mean I am to be let into the dark arts of wedding management? Molly said such things didn't concern me. Don't I just need to turn up and say yes a lot?'

'Yes, you had better turn up, Fred Archer, and yes, you had most certainly better say yes in all the right places, but I would hope you will be a bit more involved than that. Besides, with all your adoring fans, I expect everyone will be looking more at you on the big day than me!'

'That I cannot imagine. I know you will be the most breathtaking bride.'

'I hope so,' Helen answered wistfully. 'I do hope so.'

The bride-to-be didn't get very far telling Fred about the big day. The pair always had so much to say to each other they kept flitting from one subject to another. Fred was so excited about Falmouth, which was due to be finished a few days before the wedding, he couldn't help but give a full progress report. Then there was the subject of children.

'I want at least five,' Helen giggled.

'Boys and girls,' Fred agreed. 'Maybe three boys and two girls.'

'Will they all ride?' Helen inquired, teasingly.

'Of course,' confirmed Fred firmly, with an impish grin. 'Just as I did: before they can walk.'

'You're impossible!'

'We've got a dynasty of jockeys to continue,' protested her fiancé. 'Best to start as soon as possible.'

The two chatted away for the entire walk, barely noticing the magnificent countryside, despite Helen's promise her husband-to-be would enjoy it more at walking pace. By the time Fred had escorted Helen to her front door, they never did get to that wedding conversation.

'Oh dear, weren't you supposed to tell me when and where to say yes?' grinned Fred.

'Honestly, you won't get away with it that easily,' Helen chided with a mocking expression. 'My mother is holding a full rehearsal the day before the wedding and your mother will be there too. We are all invited, including you, so I suspect there will be a room full of people telling you what to do.'

'I don't mind at all. Besides, it means it is only a few hours before you are my wife. I'd go through anything for that.'

'Me too,' smiled back Helen. 'I can hardly believe it is only a few days away now. I feel like I have waited forever.'

Inevitably, the next few days flew by. In no time at all, the Dawsons and Archers were gathered in Grace Dawson's drawing room for the much anticipated dress rehearsal. It was a cold January evening and it was already dark outside. The fire crackled warmly in the grate but no one paid it any heed above the general hubbub of chatter. Molly was walking about the room with a tray filled with warm drinks and tankards of ale.

'Come along everyone,' Grace Dawson announced at the top of her voice. She was waving a thick notebook in the air. 'We've got a lot to go through.'

She didn't notice William Archer rolling his eyes and pulling Mat off to one side of the room for a quiet chat about a horse he had an eye on. Emma did, but left him to it. It was easier if he wasn't involved; besides, she had a veritable army of helpers, what with Molly and her daughters, as well as the Dawson entourage.

'It's so wonderful to have you here again,' said Mary Rose, squeezing Emma's hand as she passed on the way to her seat. 'I swear we don't see enough of each other. We must put that right now we are officially family.'

Emma smiled. She counted Mary Rose as one of her closest friends, even though they had known each other a relatively short time.

'How do you think Fred is coping?' Mary Rose asked in a quiet voice.

'He's in control, I think,' Emma whispered back. 'Everyone has looked out for him so well. Your husband sent him off today on his beloved Scotch Pearl and he seemed to be so much happier when he returned. Molly has been wonderful and been running his affairs with such kindness and efficiency. I do believe that when Helen becomes mistress Molly will sigh with relief though.'

Mary Rose giggled. Grace, who was addressing the room, interrupted their conversation by beginning to run through her list.

'Goodness me,' whispered Emma, 'this really does sound like a grand affair.'

Mary Rose nodded.

'In our world, it will be one of the events of the year. No wonder Grace is being so particular.'

Grace was now going onto describe the order of the procession between the church and the reception, which was to be held at Warren House. Suddenly she was interrupted by an urgent and loud knock at the front door.

Molly tutted and hurried out of the room and down the hallway to answer it, almost being bowled over as the caller burst through, heading in the opposite direction. It was Jack, one of the older stable lads.

'Got to see the master,' he said breathlessly, as he hurtled towards the drawing room, tipping his cap at Molly almost as an afterthought.

The room was utterly silent as Jack raced through the door and then stood stock still for a moment, his eyes darting around the room to locate Mat Dawson.

'Sir, sir, you have to come quick,' Jack said, gasping for breath.

The enormity of his situation within the social gathering then seemed to hit him and he looked a little embarrassed.

'If you can, please, and I am so sorry for interrupting. It is a bit of an emergency, see.'

'What is it Jack?' Mat said, stepping forward. He looked a little bemused.

'The ox, you know, the one Lord Hastings sent as a wedding gift? Well, it has escaped and charged up the high street. Joe was down there. He said folk were scattering all over the place. It ran all the way up to the side of the Rutland Arms.'

'He must have heard that's where the reception is going to be!' chimed in William Archer.

The room erupted into laughter. Poor Jack, he looked utterly confused now. He couldn't understand why all these folk were laughing so heartily at such a calamity.

'More likely he got wind that this was his last hour on earth,' John Dawson chortled.

'Ladies, I wonder if you would excuse the menfolk?' John continued, trying now to put on a serious face. 'I can't help believing our time would be better spent rounding up this fugitive. If we don't, our wedding breakfast will be short of a key ingredient.'

Grace smiled and nodded.

'And Freddie too?' Mat said hopefully.

'And Freddie too,' Grace nodded, shaking her head with mock anger.

The menfolk didn't need telling twice and left the room in a rowdy, back-slapping and chortling bunch within seconds. The moment the door slammed behind them, the house lapsed into silence. Grace looked from Emma to Molly and then Mary Rose and

Helen. Everyone was smiling and shaking their heads. Suddenly the whole room erupted into laughter.

'I am going to take this as a good omen,' giggled Helen.

'I think getting all the men out of the room while we get on with the real business is always a good omen,' confirmed Mary Rose.

The women laughed some more. It took a good while indeed to settle everyone down and work through the remainder of Grace's list.

Tuesday 30th January, 1883, was a day like no other in Newmarket and it was talked about for years after. All the inns and public houses were full of folk wanting to catch a glimpse of their hero on the horse and see the sweet maiden who had stolen his heart. Those who could claim to have met her were much in demand and would tell stories of what a wonderful woman she was and how kind she could be.

'Helen is one of us,' they'd nod sagely. 'She always has time to stop and chatter to everyone. She knows a fair bit about horses too.'

This would elicit a nod of approval and it was generally understood Helen was a suitable match for 'their Fred'.

Of this fact, Fred had no doubt. On the morning of the wedding, the young jockey showed no trace of nerves. Charlie, who was helping him get ready in the recently completed Falmouth House, was amazed.

'Well brother, only a few hours for you left to call it off,' he joked.

The pair had grown very close since the death of

William Junior.

'No Charlie, I have made my mind up,' Fred said, adjusting his tie. 'Helen is the one for me. Of that, I have no doubts whatsoever.'

Charlie patted his brother on the back.

'Thank goodness for that, otherwise there would be a riot in town. I cannot tell you how many are lining the streets already. We've never seen anything like it. I am glad you did not invite your friend the Royal Highness, the Prince, he would have never got through. Mind you, I am not sure how all your other VIP patrons will either!'

They both laughed. They were looking out of the large window across the yard at Fred's beautiful stables. They were always clean, but today they looked especially spotless. Fred knew that his friend Joe had personally overseen this exercise. Fred looked over to his beloved Scotch Pearl whose head was visible at his stable door and smiled to himself.

Catching his gaze, Charlie dug his brother in the ribs.

'No racing for a few weeks now, Freddie. You and Helen will have such a wonderful time though.'

'Yes I know that.' Fred nodded. Then he looked serious. 'I don't mean to be ungrateful, but I will be so glad when today is over. I am not good at crowds looking at me. Well, not while I am not on a horse anyhow.'

'Oh don't worry. I really do believe it is Helen they are here to see this time. Her dress has been the talk of every newspaper for the last few weeks. Everyone wants to know what it is like.'

Fred nodded. He knew his brother was right. Even this made him worry though. How would his fiancée cope with all the attention? It didn't seem fair. He'd grown up with it and it had become part of the territory.

'Dear Helen, she has had lots to put up with,' Fred mused. 'She just seems to take it in her stride, never getting flustered by anything, bless her. No more talk now. Let me go and enjoy the happiest day of my life.' Charlie went over to his brother and gave him a hug.

'There you are, brother, just in case I cannot get near you for the rest of the day. Mind you, I do have the ring, so you had better not lose me altogether.'

'Thank goodness for that,' Fred smiled at his brother. 'How dear Will would have enjoyed today, hey Charlie? Let's be sure to raise a glass to him later.'

With one final check in the mirror, the brothers headed out of the room. Molly was waiting at the bottom of the stairs and shrieked when she saw them.

'Boys, you look so handsome and grown up,' she exclaimed. 'Oh dear, I swore I wouldn't cry. Now look at me, blubbing away like a newborn.' Fred hurried towards her and swept her up in a big hug.

'Now Molly, contain yourself,' chided Fred. 'I can't help remembering another wedding not so many years ago when I had to say no tears. What is it with you and these big days?'

Molly was laughing and crying at the same time now.

'I must say,' Fred added, 'Molly you look as pretty as a picture. If you were not married to Bert, and I about to marry Helen, it would most certainly be you, Molly.'

'Oh Freddie, what a grand man you have become. To me though, you'll always be just my dear, dear Freddie.'

Charlie interrupted the good friends.

'Come on, it is time to get into the carriage. Are Bert, Joe, and Sam all in there already Molly?'

'Yes, my darling, they are all there waiting.'

The brothers said a fond farewell and hurried outside. Molly's husband and Fred's two closest friends turned to the brothers and cheered. Fred and Charlie climbed on board to join them and there was much shaking of hands and back-slapping.

'My goodness Freddie boy, you scrub up well,' joked Sam.

'You look dressed for a wedding,' chimed in Joe. 'Who is the unlucky maiden?'

'There is a queue of four-legged fillies that swear he is theirs,' Sam said, pretending to look mystified. 'There will be some exceptionally long faces in the stables if it is not one of them.'

'That is enough, boys,' Fred chortled. 'If we carry on like this, we'll be later than the bride.'

Bert nodded and leaned forward to speak to the carriage driver.

'Freddie is right,' he said, turning to the others. 'It's going to be tough making our way through the crowds. They were standing six deep on the way here and I could see more people joining at the back.'

The carriage moved off slowly, the wood and leather creaking with the effort of the movement. The men in the carriage waved frantically at Molly and Bert blew his wife a kiss.

'See you at the church,' he called.

'Good luck,' she shouted back, but didn't hear the reply. As the carriage went through the gates of Falmouth House, the cheer that went up was deafening. Fred was used to crowds at his race meetings but he had never seen anything like this. There were upturned faces as far as he could see. Some were waving hats, others pieces of fabric, riding crops, or anything that came to hand really.

As the carriage made its way down the streets, there never once seemed to be a break in the crowd. Everyone seemed to be straining to take a look and there was a cacophony of shouts of, 'There he is!' repeated again and again as they travelled forward. Fred was dumbstruck. He knew there would be crowds, but never once did he imagine that there would be so many people.

Charlie squeezed his arm.

'You didn't expect this did you?' he shouted over the din. 'They love you. Everyone knows you as a quiet, unassuming jockey that has time for all folk. That's why they are here.

'Imagine what it will be like for dear Helen who has all this to see in a short while. I hope her nerves are steadier than yours.'

Fred looked momentarily alarmed, but once he thought it through he relaxed.

'She's made of tougher stuff than me,' Fred said. 'She will be as shocked as I am, but I expect someone has warned her. She'll love seeing all those happy faces.'

In no time at all, they arrived at the church. The crowd let out an extra loud cheer as they got down from the carriage. The group walked slowly up the path, greeting folk and thanking them for coming. When they finally arrived at the church doors, the vicar was waiting for them. He shook Fred warmly by the hand and then each of his companions in turn. The vicar led them inside and the guests, already settled in their pews, all turned to see the groom's arrival, their heads swivelling around as they followed his progress up the aisle.

Now he was in the church, Fred felt suddenly calm. All the faces he could see now were friends and family members. They were people that meant so much to him, and now Helen too. The jockey's heart began to beat normally and when he caught sight of his father and mother he broke into a broad smile. He was no longer nervous or unsure. All he wanted was for the doors to open again and for Helen to be there.

He heard a huge roar of the crowd outside. She was here. His heart began to beat loudly in his chest once again. He looked over to Charlie, who smiled and patted his top pocket which held the ring.

This was finally it.

Fred gasped when he saw Helen standing at the door, standing beside her father John. She looked beautiful. Her dress was perfect; a Princessline, satin, fitted bodice and skirt, covered with intricate and flowing antique Venetian lace. The off-white creation hung off her delicate frame in gentle folds, shimmering in the bright light. She wore a simple veil held in place by a garland of orange blossom. Fred smiled to himself as he saw his wife-to-be reach up and nervously fiddle with a brooch. It was none other than the diamond horseshoe brooch he had given her a few days before as a surprise wedding present. He had hidden a small note in the box and wondered if she had seen it today.

It said: *'To my soon-to-be wife, this is the happiest day of my life.'*

The strains of Mendelssohn's Wedding March struck up and Helen began her journey up the aisle, followed by her pretty bridesmaids all dressed in coral-coloured silk dresses with matching orange blossom garlands in their hair and bracelets of diamonds and pearls on their wrists.

No one was really looking at the girls though. All eyes were on Helen, who seemed to float down the aisle. She was breathtakingly beautiful.

Helen did not look left or right, but looked straight ahead at her beloved Freddie who was standing there smiling at her. She barely registered the crowds, or heard the 'aahs' of the congregation, or the wonderful glow of the candles, or the sweet scent of the flowers that filled the air. When, at last, she reached Fred's side, she smiled at her father and put out her hand to her fiancé who gently took it and smiled down at her. The service began.

Outside, the crowd waited patiently and, after what seemed an age, they could hear the sounds of muffled cheering and the Wedding March once again. A few moments later, the church bells started to peal. The crowd went wild, cheering and clapping, and when the church doors swung open to reveal the new Mr and Mrs Fred Archer the noise was unbelievable. The newlyweds held hands and were smiling broadly. They really were a picture.

The crowd went even more wild as the pair made their way down the church path. It was slow progress because they stopped to thank the onlookers as they went and the people bobbed and weaved in a desperate attempt to get close to the Archers. The women all wanted to tell Helen how beautiful she was in her dress and the men all wanted to shake Fred's hand.

Fred and Helen giggled as cloud after cloud of rice was thrown in their direction.

'Well done!' shouted the crowd.

'Congratulations!'

'Good luck!'

It took a very long time indeed before Fred and Helen reached their carriage, but they were careful to betray no sense of impatience. These people had waited a long time to see them and they were just as an important part of the celebrations as everyone else.

Yet another cloud of rice appeared as they climbed into the carriage, accompanied by a spontaneous round of applause. A man in the crowd called for three cheers for the happy couple and everyone obliged at the top of their voices. The carriage set off with a creak and a groan, making for Warren House where Helen's parents had a feast laid out for the wedding breakfast. The newlyweds waved at the crowds that lined the route all the way there.

'Gosh, I am going to be exhausted by the end of today,' Helen whispered to her husband.

'You can't flag yet,' he whispered back. 'We're only at the start of this race!'

He was right too. Grace had also arranged a ball at the Rutland Arms for family and close friends to follow the wedding breakfast and then Fred and Helen had promised to drop into various other parties that were being held in their honour, including one for all the stable lads at Heath House. No one was to be left out.

Back at the church, William and Emma thanked the vicar and greeted as many guests as they could, as did Mat, Grace, and John Dawson. After a long while, the crowds began to drift off, keen to get to whatever celebration they'd wrangled a place at afterwards.

Emma was looking over at her husband who was in deep conversation with Mat and Lord Falmouth, when she heard a familiar voice at her shoulder.

'May I be the first to congratulate you on such a wonderful service?'

She swung round and smiled at Lord James. He looked very handsome in his morning suit and top hat.

'Edward,' she breathed, blushing slightly, despite herself.

'I do not think I have ever seen a church look so warm and welcoming,' he said, lifting her hand and brushing his lips against it lightly. 'They look a fine couple, Emma. You must be so proud. I know I am. I mean, well, to have such a special relationship with your son and Helen is perfect.'

'Thank you Edward,' Emma said, slowly withdrawing her hand and looking about her. 'I am in awe of the folk that have turned out. Have you ever seen so many? I am so glad you could come here to witness their wedding.'

Lord James broke into a smile.

'I would travel across the globe if it meant the opportunity to spend a few hours in your company,' he said quietly. 'This is just the icing on the cake.'

For a few moments the pair simply stared at one another. Emma felt for a brief, tantalising few seconds as though all the crowds had simply evaporated and it was only the two of them in the world. Forcing herself to look away, she looked over at the figures retreating towards the carriages.

'We must go, they'll be waiting,' she said, her voice cracking with emotion.

'Can I ask one favour then? You will at least do me the honour of dancing with me this evening.'

Emma allowed herself to look back at Lord James and nodded slowly. How could she resist the opportunity of just a few minutes of close contact with this man? She knew it was wrong, but she couldn't help herself. God knows she would be cursed for it though.

'Ah, Mr Dawson, wonderful service, don't you think,' said Lord James tearing his eyes away from

Emma. He'd seen Mat approaching out of the corner of his eye and immediately stepped forward to intercept him.

'Why thank you Lord James, but I can't accept any praise,' said Mat, taking the outstretched hand and shaking it warmly. 'The ladies did all the hard work.'

'They are a wonder, aren't they?' Lord James said, casting one last glance at Emma as he set off towards the carriages, chatting animatedly to Mat Dawson.

Left momentarily alone, Emma sighed.

'Come on, Em.'

William's voice made her jump. She hadn't seen him coming over.

'You look a bit in shock, love. Must be all the excitement of the day. Let me help you up onto our carriage. It is time we held a glass in our hand and got that dancing started.'

Emma smiled at her husband and took his arm. She thought back to her own wedding day. It wasn't nearly as grand as this, but William was a good man. He'd always done his best.

She leaned into him and gave him a peck on the cheek.

'What is that for?' he grinned. 'You getting all carried away with the wedding?'

'Maybe,' she laughed. 'Or maybe I just don't pay you enough heed. I love you, William Archer, and if Fred and Helen are as content as we have been together, they are going to do alright.'

CHAPTER SEVEN

Fred and Helen stood no chance of slipping away quietly from their wedding reception. Even though the band was playing a catchy tune and the dance floor was crowded with laughing couples swaying to the music, the moment Fred and Helen began to move towards the exit a great roar went up through the crowd.

'The lovebirds are off!' someone cried.

'You got somewhere better to be?' joked another.

The music died down as the crowds surged forward to say their goodbyes.

'Good luck my darlings,' Emma said, taking one of each of Helen and Fred's hands and squeezing them tight. 'Look after each other. You are a perfect couple.'

'Yeah, you look after that young lassie,' slurred William Archer, swaying slightly, spilling a little ale from the tankard which had been permanently gripped tightly in his hand all afternoon. 'And don't do anything I wouldn't do. We will need you back for the new season.'

'William, they are only away for two weeks,' Emma said, shooting a withering glance at her husband, but it creased into a soft smile when she saw him stagger backwards only to be helped to keep upright by Mat Dawson.

'Just don't get too distracted by the bright lights of London,' Mat joked. 'We need you back here as soon as possible.'

Fred smiled. Meanwhile, in the background, a volley of comments was being made wishing him and his new bride good luck.

'I'll be back, sir, don't you worry,' he said. 'This is where I, no, *we*, belong.'

Taking Helen firmly by the hand, he pushed his way gently but determinedly through the cheering crowd, heading towards the carriage which would take them to the train station. More clouds of rice appeared.

'Where are they getting all that rice from?' Helen whispered to her husband. 'You could feed a large family for a year on the amount that has been thrown today!'

Fred laughed.

'You're not wrong there, my darling. Here we are now, let me help you in.'

Helen hopped up into the carriage and her husband followed her.

'Alone at last,' she giggled.

'Well, almost,' smiled back Fred.

The crowd that surrounded the carriage were now thumping their hands on the side of it in time with their cheering. The din was tremendous.

'Are they ever going to get tired of following us around?' Fred said, in mock exasperation.

'Following you around, you mean. Mind you, I don't blame them. I'd follow you everywhere too.'

'Ah, well *you* have to follow me,' Fred grinned. 'That's what all those "yeses" and "I dos" were about today. You are now officially never allowed to leave my side.'

'I can't argue with that,' Helen said, snuggling up closer to Fred. 'I wouldn't want to break any official rules.'

The crowd lined the route to the train station, just as they had done to the church and cheered them all the way into their First Class carriage. As the train steamed out of the station, the newlyweds leaned out of the window and waved. The crowd responded with even louder shouts and cheers, which Fred and Helen could still hear clearly long after the sight of the crowd had receded into the far distance.

'Gosh, I don't think I will ever get used to all those people watching me all the time,' Helen said, as they both sank into their seats. 'How do you ever manage it?'

'Don't be silly. You are a natural.'

'No I am not. It makes me so nervous. I am sure people must see it and wonder at what a silly goose you've married. Mind you, that is nothing to how nervous I was when I got to the church today. I had to fix my gaze onto your eyes and concentrate like mad or I would have fainted on the spot. Poor Father said afterwards he would have bruises on his arm for a week where I was hanging on so tight.'

'But you still enjoyed it though?'

'Of course I did.'

'Good, and it is not over yet. We've got time in London, Cornwall, and France to go yet. I feel like we are royalty, doing some sort of European tour.'

'I don't mind where we go, just so long as we are together.'

Fred squeezed Helen tightly. He couldn't believe how lucky he was to have found a woman like Helen. He loved her so deeply. She was quite unlike any other woman he had ever met.

Fred had always been attractive to women. His success on the racecourse, coupled with his brooding, dark good looks were an aphrodisiac to ladies, many of whom pursued him quite openly, even though some of them were already married. Fred's polite charm as he refused their embellishments only served to make him seem more attractive. They'd twitter and preen and follow him, but he never seemed to notice.

Helen, on the other hand, seemed so different. Intellectually, she was his equal. She knew and cared about the same things that he did and always instinctively knew the right thing to say. It was not for her to worry about superficial fripperies such as hair and make-up, although she was quite exquisite to look at. She'd be much more interested in discussing the form of a particular horse, or to understand new advances in veterinary practice.

With Helen at his side, Fred felt like anything was possible. Her support and encouragement gave him an inner strength and confidence he never knew he had.

On their return from honeymoon, the atmosphere around Fred and Helen was as frantic as ever. They got the distinct impression the celebrations had continued apace in their absence and they showed no signs of abating. Helen did her best to get on with settling into their newly built home, Falmouth House, but it wasn't easy with constant visitors and interruptions. Neither she nor Fred really minded though. They were so happy and in a world of their own anyhow.

Everyone had noticed the change in Fred. Where previously he rarely smiled, he now laughed and joked all the time. There was a lightness in his step that made people want to be around him more than ever. None of this was to say he lost his focus when it came to racing. If anything, he was more focussed than ever. He watched everything around him, took in every detail and soaked up information more than ever before. The difference was, now he seemed to love every second of his life.

'I really do not think we can fit in any more trophies, or pictures, dearest Freddie,' Helen chided her husband. It was now more than three months after their honeymoon and she was still in the throes of unpacking. 'The drawing room is full, so is your study and I have just taken up the last space in the hall. Perhaps you might like to ask your mother and father to take a few to the hotel? The two public bar areas have many newspaper cuttings of you up on the walls already. They would probably love to have some of your prize pictures. This is only if you agree, my love.'

Helen turned to face Fred and found that, yet again, he was simply standing there staring at her.

'Are you listening to me?' she laughed.

'No, yes, well, sort of,' he smiled. 'Do whatever you feel is right. You always know best.'

Helen smiled back.

'Fine, I shall speak to your mother. I think it would be right to give Molly and Bert a few things too, don't you think? They've been so good to us. Gosh, there is so much to do.'

The newlyweds' wonderful new home brought them both great pleasure. Falmouth House was opulent and very spacious, with a long dining room, spacious drawing room, breakfast room, conservatory and even a private, two-roomed Turkish bath for Fred. In the cellar there were two hundred bottles of champagne and fine wines.

Helen loved to entertain and had arranged a seemingly never-ending stream of evenings with friends shortly after their return. They had so many people to thank and enjoyed sharing their good fortune with loved ones. They employed a good cook and plenty of helping hands for all the visitors that arrived day and night.

'What are your plans for today, Helen?' Fred said, as he walked over to the fire and threw another log onto the embers.

It was early May and the long cold, wet spring

which never seemed to want to end was continuing to cause havoc in the yards and in town too. Thank goodness the weather had been kind during their wedding in January. It was certainly making up for it now.

'I really advise against going out, the roads are terrible,' Fred added.

'No, don't worry Freddie. Molly and I are going to go through all the wedding gifts that still need to be put where we want them, so she will be here soon. Later on, the family are all coming for lunch and I know my sisters are keen to play draughts with you. Do you think you will be able to join us?'

'Tell Lillie and Annie to watch out,' Fred laughed. 'I can't be beaten. Not today, not ever!'

They both laughed. Helen did so love that look of determination that crossed Fred's face whenever he competed at anything. He really, really didn't like to lose.

'Right, I have to go and speak with Joe. I will see you all later.'

Fred gave Helen a peck on the cheek and left the room, only to run into Molly.

'Hello Freddie,' she exclaimed, smiling broadly. 'My, isn't it cold? My poor Bert is really struggling with the yard today.'

'Hello Molly,' Fred smiled, stooping to give her a peck on the cheek. 'Does he need more help? I could send for Sam and he will get some extra lads in.'

'Oh, would you, pet? Bert told me last night that the horses are so restless, what with not going out.

These last four weeks must have been the wettest start to spring ever.'

'I will sort it straight away, Molly. Helen is in the drawing room waiting for you. See you later.'

Fred soon caught up with Joe, who was waiting for him in his study, as arranged. Joe was in and out of Falmouth House every day. Fred relied on him increasingly because the pressure around him seemed to be growing greater all the time. After being promoted to become Mat Dawson's partner, Fred now had to help supervise the stables and its large team of apprentices. There were acres of paperwork to help with in order to record the entries and placings of their horses. Fred also had to be constantly on hand with advice or comment, or to ride out to give his opinion on a horse. While Mat Dawson adored Fred and respected him hugely, he would not let him rest and as Fred's old master grew older, he became ever more reliant on his one-time protégé.

Today, Fred and Joe were studying the layout of Falmouth House, to see if they could fit in another few stables at one end. Freddie didn't want the stable area to be too big, but was thinking ahead to when he retired from racing and would manage the next generation of jockeys full-time. Of course, the weather was not helping, holding up the building work they had already started.

They were just discussing whether or not to bring in more builders in order to move the job along, when Fred lost his train of thought completely. His voice trailed off and he stared out the window to the yard outside.

'Are you OK?' Joe asked, following the direction of his gaze. 'You seem a little distracted today.'

'I was just thinking,' Fred said. His tone was unusually serious. 'Did you hear about all the burglaries? Bert was telling me about them yesterday. There were a number while Helen and I were away and another few in the past few months since we've been back.'

'Oh, don't worry about all that,' Joe said, with a dismissive swipe of his hand. 'There are always so many people here all the time, it would be a brave burglar indeed that tried to break into Falmouth. Besides, if one did get in, I don't rate his chances against Molly. She'd have his guts for garters!'

They both laughed.

'All the same though,' said Fred, becoming serious again. 'I'd hate for anything to happen, especially with Helen.'

Joe nodded. He knew how much his friend felt for his wife.

'Do you remember that revolver I was given? You know, when I won the Liverpool Cup on Sterling. Thomas Roughton, the owner was so happy and grateful, he presented me with it afterwards.'

'Yes, I remember,' said Joe, frowning slightly. 'It was a bit of an odd gift. I thought that at the time. What's wrong with a handsome tip? Why do you mention it now?'

'I've put it in the drawer beside my bed. For safety.'

'Are you sure that is wise?' said his friend, very concerned now. 'Do you even know how to use it properly?'

'Of course I do. It is just a precaution. Don't worry about it. In fact, forget I mentioned it. Besides, I have something much more important to talk about.'

Joe looked at his friend intently, waiting to hear what he had to say. He expected it would be about a forthcoming race, or a horse he fancied.

'We need to think about preparing for a very important new apprentice,' Fred said.

Joe looked at him, not really understanding what he was getting at.

'He won't be ready to ride for a few years, but I believe he has a glittering career in front of him if he is to achieve the family legacy…'

Joe stared at Fred and then suddenly a look of recognition bloomed across his face.

'What? You mean… is Helen with child? Oh my goodness, that is incredible news.'

Joe leapt to his feet and grabbed Fred's hand, pumping it up and down.

'Congratulations.'

Fred smiled.

'We are so happy,' Fred smiled. 'I can't believe we have been so fortunate. You mustn't tell anyone for now. Helen wants to tell John and Grace in her own time and you know how these things are. I just wanted you to know. I had to tell someone.'

Everything seemed set for another wonderful year for Fred Archer. Helen was pregnant with their first child and the two were eagerly awaiting this fantastic event. The week before, Fred had won the Two Thousand Guineas on a horse called Galliard, in a race with a nail-biting finish. The newly widowed Duchess of Montrose had also recently returned to the scene, offering Fred pretty much a blank cheque to retain his services as a jockey. She'd been left an immense fortune by her recently deceased second husband W.S. Stirling Crawfurd and was very obviously infatuated by Fred. Fred, who still had many demands on his purse, and even more so now he had a large house to run, demurred, gallantly pretending to barely notice how much the elderly lady flirted and preened in his presence.

'I really do feel like I am fulfilling all my life dreams,' Fred told Joe. 'It's like nothing could ever go wrong for me ever again.'

'I'm very pleased to hear that.'

'Do you remember that time we went to that fair? It was six years ago, we were up north and I had just had my 218th win. We decided to have our fortunes told and that gypsy told me death and sadness was coming to me.'

'I remember it well,' Joe nodded. 'I don't know why you listen to that nonsense though.'

'I always wondered if she'd seen what would happen to William Junior. Then, after Will died, I wondered if that was it. Whether there was any more death and sadness to come. Now I think it is done. In fact, I am sure of it. Everything is going to be fine.'

'You think about things far too deeply,' Joe said. 'I reckon folk with a gift like yours often do. They think, why me? Why am I so lucky to be given this gift? Just remember though, you work for it and you deserve everything you have got. This job of yours drives you beyond the limits of human endurance and we know it can bring on flights of fear, depression, and self-doubt.

'Do me a favour my friend, don't listen to fortune tellers. You've told me today that you are the happiest you have ever been. Enjoy it and live for the moment. You have worked for it.'

'Thank you Joe. You've got a wise head on those shoulders. Now, let's get these plans finished.'

What Fred didn't know then was how short-lived his happiness would be. His life was about to take a significant turn for the worse.

It all started innocently enough. Fred was to ride Galliard in the derby, following their successful pairing in the Two Thousand Guineas. This time though, he was up against his brother Charles who was on Highland Chief. Charles, like Fred, had a habit of gambling on his own rides and this time was no exception. Indeed, he was so convinced of Highland Chief's chances, he put on a huge bet. It was so significant, he stood to lose £1,000 if the horse didn't win and he didn't hold back from sharing this with his brother. If Fred was concerned, he didn't say anything. In his own mind, he always raced to win and this time was no exception. He couldn't allow his focus to be clouded by his profligate sibling.

Galliard was the clear favourite at odds of 100-30, but Fred was worried about his ride. When she was exercised prior to the race she was behaving in an uncharacteristically temperamental and highly strung way, working up a terrific sweat.

'Do you think we should pull out?' Fred asked Mat Dawson. 'This doesn't look good.'

Fred was still seated on Galliard and Mat was examining the horse.

'I think he is OK, but he needs to settle. I am going to speak to the stewards and ask if we can give the pre-race parade a skip. Give me a few moments. I will signal to you if it is alright and you take him to the start.'

Fred nodded and Mat headed off to the stewards' enclosure. After a few minutes he emerged and waved Fred on towards the start line. Fred tipped his hat in acknowledgement, dug his heels into Galliard's side and headed towards the start line.

If Fred had heard the conversations that went on in the enclosure at that moment, he would have been very worried indeed. Race-goers were very upset at the favourite's absence. It was virtually unheard of to have no sight of the favourite before a race. Rumours swirled around that there was something not quite right about that year's derby.

Nevertheless, the race began well for the Archer boys and Galliard seemed to have recovered from his earlier flightiness. They rode hard and pretty soon there were just three horses in the race, Galliard, Highland Chief, and another hotly tipped horse called St Blaise. With Fred's horse putting his brother's one under pressure, the Archer boys managed to give St Blaise a real race as the three of them thundered towards the finishing post leaving the rest of the field trailing in their wake. The crowd roared as the three battled it out, neck and neck. Then, at the final moment, Highland Chief and St Blaise surged forward, leaving Galliard half a neck behind at the finish.

The judges gave first place to St Blaise, with Highland Chief second and Galliard in third.

The horses had barely got to the paddock before the rumours that emerged before the race turned into a clamour of ugly unrest. It was well known the Archer brothers were close and since Charles had been a little too open about the amount of money he had backed his horse with, people started to add two and two together. Whether or not they made four is another question, but race-goers certainly believed Fred had eased off on Galliard to give his brother a break.

Fred Archer, for so long the most popular jockey on the circuit, was for the first time in his life regarded with suspicion and distrust. Many people passionately believed that if he had given his all and thrown himself at the finish, he would have clinched it. They said he simply wasn't trying out of loyalty to his sibling.

The descent grew at a dizzying rate. It wasn't long before open accusations of Fred throwing the race were being made in newspapers. Fred was devastated. In his heart of hearts he knew he had given his all for that race. There was no way he would ever have eased up out of loyalty to his brother, however deeply he loved him. Their father had taught them well. They knew the only way to succeed on the racetrack was to be utterly ruthless.

The pure and simple truth was Galliard was not fit for the race. He and Mat had had their doubts ahead of the race and they should have gone with their gut feelings.

Fred had never felt so wretched in his life. The sudden change in mood from the elation that followed the honeymoon and the news of the impending birth, to the accusations and mistrust that followed the derby were almost too much to bear. Meanwhile, Fred felt under pressure to present a strong front for Helen's sake. Although she said everything was fine, it was obvious she was not finding her pregnancy easy. Now she was in her final few months, she looked permanently pale and uncomfortable.

Unable to speak of his concerns to Helen, because he didn't want to worry her, Fred penned a long and emotional letter to his mother. He began by saying he hoped that she, and his father, were not disturbed at the rumours and accusations swirling around him and his brother and assured her, if any assurance were needed, there was no truth in them. He went on to write movingly of his fears for the future and concerns over Helen and then chided himself for worrying Emma unduly.

'Helen's mother Grace is here all the time, but she looks as exhausted as Helen,' Fred wrote. *'I just worry that things are not going as they should.'*

The day Emma received the letter, she packed her bags and headed off to Falmouth House. Emily, who was also frantic with worry, joined her.

'You are in charge,' Emma instructed her husband before they left, saying it in a way where William

Archer immediately knew there was no point in arguing. 'Freddie needs us. Helen too.'

When mother and daughter arrived at Falmouth House, they were shocked at the change there. On their last visit the house was light and bright and full of laughter, now the atmosphere was dark and subdued. Fred looked tired and his deep brown eyes had uncharacteristically dark patches below them. He looked like he hadn't slept for days. He was also listless and yet seemed to have no idea what to do with himself. Helen, on the other hand, seemed to be trying to be everywhere at once, sorting everything out in the household, even though she plainly found each step painful to make. Grace too was everywhere and anywhere, running herself ragged.

The Archer ladies immediately took charge.

'Helen, you look exhausted,' Emma ordered. 'I want you to go and take a nap right now. You too, Grace. We'll sort out everything here. Now come on, be off with you.'

While Emily took Grace for a sit down, Emma ushered Helen upstairs and helped her into bed. Closing the heavy drapes she noticed with satisfaction that her daughter-in-law had already closed her eyes. Poor love. She looked terrible.

Emma let herself quietly out of the room and returned to find her son pacing up and down the drawing room.

'Well, it is lovely to see you Freddie, but I can't help wondering why you are indoors on a lovely day like this. Aren't you needed in the yard?'

Fred shook his head.

'Everything is fine there, I, I…' His voice trailed off.

'Well, I think we need to get a nice cup of tea inside you and you can sit and tell me what is happening. I am quite sure this is the first time ever you couldn't be tempted outside to your precious horses.'

Fred smiled, but it was a small, tense smile that didn't spread to his eyes. He was so happy to see his mother, but didn't know where to start. How could he explain that he hardly dared compete again after the derby? He didn't even feel up to exercising a horse.

Emma sensed his reluctance to talk and immediately switched to keep the subject matter light. She knew her son well enough by now to know there was no use in pushing him when he didn't want to talk about something. Instead, she amused him with the latest goings on at their hotel and all the antics of William Archer.

'Honestly, he is the living end. You'll never guess what he did last week…'

She knew Fred was only half listening. At least though he had stopped pacing the room.

That evening, Emma wrote a long letter to Lord James. She told him what was happening at Falmouth House and how Fred was in the throes of utter misery.

'…You know I trust your judgement entirely,' she wrote. 'I feel so desperate and alone here. I need to help my beloved Freddie and Helen, but I hardly know what to do. I feel he needs to start riding again, but he has lost all interest in horses and mopes about like a widower…'

Lord James could not ignore Emma's entreaties. He never could. As soon as he received the letter, he too headed towards Falmouth House.

He never said a word to Fred about Emma's letter. Lord James simply said he needed Fred's urgent advice on a horse.

'As luck would have it, it is not half a day's ride from here,' he said to Fred. 'Is there any chance you could come with me today and see it? I would be indebted.'

'I've not ridden for a while,' Fred said, somewhat weakly. 'I could perhaps ask Joe?'

'No, no, it has to be you, old chap,' Lord James said earnestly. 'I've just got a feeling about this one and you've always been spot on in the past.'

'Go on Freddie,' encouraged Emma. 'I'm going to be here, so Helen will be fine with me. By the looks of you, you could do with some fresh air. You'll be back by this evening.'

Fred hesitated and then nodded.

'Great news,' said Lord James, clapping his hands loudly together and giving Emma a subtle wink. 'I'll ask the lads to get the horses saddled up and ready and you meet me in the yard.'

'Thank you,' Emma mouthed to Lord James, as Fred got up and walked purposefully out of the room.

Lord James crossed the room and picked up Emma's hand and lightly brushed it with his lips. A familiar surge of electricity passed between them.

'You know I am always there for you. You only ever have to ask.'

'Thank you Edward,' she breathed.

Emma didn't move for a long while after Lord James left the room. In the distance she heard the sound of the two men setting off and the house was plunged into silence. The only noise she could hear was the racing of her heart. She was so grateful to Lord James. He always seemed to make things right. If only things had been different. Emma closed her eyes to block the thoughts that crowded into her mind.

Suddenly, the silence was shattered by a piercing scream. It came from upstairs. Emma raced into the hallway and almost ran headlong into Emily who was coming from the kitchen.

'Was that Helen?' Emily said, her eyes wide.

'Yes,' said Emma, making for the large staircase. 'Go and send for the midwife and the doctor. Right now. That didn't sound good. And get Joe, or Bert, to go after Fred and Lord James. They only left ten minutes ago.'

'Right, right,' said Emily, heading towards the door.

Emma raced up the stairs. As she reached the landing there was another howl of pain. Her heart was really thumping now. *Hang on, hang on,* she thought, *help is on the way. Pray God she is all right.*

When she reached the bedroom door, she pushed it open and rushed inside. Helen was bent double in pain, surrounded by crumpled bed sheets. She was deathly pale and covered in a light sheen of sweat.

'Where does it hurt?' Emma said, hurrying over to the side of the bed.

She reached out to touch Helen's brow. It felt like it was on fire.

'I am so sorry to worry you,' Helen gulped. 'I feel so awful though. I hope my baby is all right. I am just getting the most awful pains in my back. Is this what happens?'

The younger woman's face was etched in pain and concern. Emma felt entirely helpless. She realised that although she had had five children herself, she actually had very little knowledge of childbirth. What she did know, however, was it was best to sound confident and in control.

'Right, I am going to fetch some cool towels to bring your temperature down. Emily is sending for the doctor and midwife.'

'Where is Freddie?' Helen moaned.

'And Emily is also sending someone to fetch Freddie. He's gone out riding with Lord James but he'd not long left the house. She's also gone to wake your mother too and get her back in here.'

'At least Freddie is riding again,' murmured Helen.

Just then, she must have received another spasm of pain, because her entire body went rigid.

Emily rushed into the room.

'The doctor is on his way,' she said, and then stopped short when she saw what a state Helen was in. 'And Bert reckons he can catch Fred and Lord James.'

'It'll be the first time that he'll have overtaken Freddie on a horse, I'll wager,' whispered Helen, with a weak smile.

'Aye and Molly will put him in the next Gold Cup if he does,' laughed Emily softly. 'Right, now, what can I do, Mother?'

The two ladies did their best to make Helen comfortable and were shortly joined in this endeavour by Grace. It wasn't easy because every time she had a spasm of pain, she'd throw off all the sheets they had so carefully tucked around her. After a short while, Freddie came running into the room, breathless from his fast ride.

'Helen, Helen!' he shouted. 'Please tell me you are all right?'

He looked terrified.

'She's going to be fine,' soothed Emma.

'I am,' whispered Helen, her voice growing faint. 'Please don't worry.'

'Where is that doctor?' Grace hissed. 'If Freddie can get here so quickly…'

Just then, the door flew open again and the doctor and midwife hurried in.

The doctor took one glance at the patient and immediately asked if the room could be cleared.

'Why don't you wait downstairs, Mr Archer?' he said to Fred gently. 'I expect it will be a while before there is any news.'

Emma took charge and led Freddie back down to the drawing room before organising a stiff drink to be brought to him. She then hurried back upstairs and waited patiently outside Helen's room.

After a short while, the doctor emerged and beckoned Emma to speak with him a little way down the corridor.

Speaking in a low voice, he said: 'I'm not happy with the way the baby is laying and Helen is terribly weak. I believe this will be a very difficult birth, Mrs Archer. I want you to be aware of this and to decide whether or not to convey this to Mr Archer now, or leave it and see how it progresses.'

Emma's hand flew to her mouth. This was terrible news. They were such a beautiful couple. If anything happened to the baby it would break their hearts. If anything happened to Helen, well, it didn't bear thinking about.

'I don't think I will say anything to Freddie,' Emma whispered hoarsely, trying to stop the tears that were pricking her eyes. 'He's not been in good spirits of late and will only panic. I'm sure Helen needs a calm atmosphere, don't you agree?'

The doctor nodded.

'Yes, I think that is probably wise. There is little Mr Archer could do anyhow. What I am going to do, with your permission, is to call in another colleague to give a second opinion.'

'As you wish, doctor. Please do everything you can.'

The doctor headed off downstairs to find someone to take a note to his colleague. Emma slipped into the bedroom and sat on the bed, clasping Helen's hand.

Grace held the other hand. She looked as pale and worried as Emma felt. Helen looked so weak and sick.

'Hang on, my darling, hang on,' Emma whispered. 'It will all soon be over and long forgotten. Is there anything I can get you?'

Helen shook her head.

'Emily will sit with you and Grace is here too. The doctor will be back in a moment. I am just going to pop downstairs and speak with Freddie, because you know how much he frets about you. I'll be back in a moment.'

Emma dashed off downstairs to update Freddie. She said as little as she could, but knew her son sensed something was up. He was always so sensitive and perceptive. That was part of his charm.

For the next few hours, Emma shuttled between an increasingly anxious Freddie, who was now also being kept company by Lord James, who had returned shortly after Fred from their ride, and Helen, who grew more and more weak as the night progressed.

At 1am, the two doctors and a midwife delivered a baby boy. He only ever gave off one tiny rasping cry, which Helen barely heard as she slipped into unconsciousness after losing so much blood. The doctors called for Fred to come to the room urgently. His new-born son was so pale and his breathing so shallow, they knew he could not live. They wrapped the boy, who looked perfect in every way, in a white shawl and presented him to Fred.

'Helen will be fine, but I am afraid your son is very sick,' the doctor said gently. 'We tried to save him, but there is nothing we can do.'

Tears fell down the jockey's cheeks as he took the baby and stared at this wonderful, yet tragic sight. He staggered slightly and fell into a chair beside the fire, still holding the tiny, lifeless bundle. He realised with a start the baby had died in his arms.

Fred looked up at his mother. His expression was so lost and helpless, Emma thought her heart would break. She would have given anything to take away the pain her son felt.

'I'm so sorry,' she whispered. 'The doctors did everything they could.'

Fred sat like this for a few moments until Emily stepped forward and very carefully took the baby out of his arms.

Almost mechanically, Fred stood up and walked over to the bed. He knelt down and picked up Helen's hand, kissing each of her fingers one by one. He didn't say a word. When he had finished, he rested his head on the bed and gave a huge choking sob.

Helen's eyes fluttered open and she looked over at her husband. Large tears fell down her cheeks.

'Our baby?' she whispered.

Fred shook his head slowly.

'He's gone,' he said quietly.

The howl that came out of Helen's mouth shook the whole house. No one in the room that day could help but wonder how this lovely young couple could ever get through such a tragedy.

CHAPTER EIGHT

The funeral was a quiet, family affair. William joined his wife Emma and their daughter Emily, and they were accompanied to the church by Helen's parents John and Grace, as well as Molly and Bert and Mary Rose and Mat. Helen and Fred wanted it to be as low key as possible. It wouldn't have been respectful to William Junior to have crowds of onlookers outside, craning their heads for a look at the famous couple.

It was hard to believe that this church had been the scene of so much happiness at their wedding less than a year before. Fred and Helen sat close together, their hands tightly clasped as they stared at the tiny coffin. Their expressions said it all. The pain was unbearable.

When the service was over, the small party returned to Falmouth House for the wake. Although Molly had seen to it that quite a spread was laid on, no one had much of an appetite.

'Are you alright, Helen?' Emma asked, concern

etched on her face. 'You have to eat, my dear. You need to keep your strength up.'

'I know,' Helen said, doing her best to smile, but barely managed to raise the corner of her pretty rosebud lips. 'I just…'

'What, my darling? You can talk to me. We've both lost a son, perhaps I can be of help.'

Helen took a deep breath, as though she was struggling to articulate something.

'I know this sounds silly, because my William Junior barely had time in this world, but I can't get over how quiet this house is now,' she said quietly. 'I think I spent so long imagining how it would be filled with the sound of the laughter of our child, and yes probably howls too, this whole place feels empty now. It is as though Falmouth is in mourning too.'

Emma nodded. She completely understood the emptiness that went with losing a child. One's imagination can make things a lot harder.

'I think you need to spend some time away from here,' Emma said. 'To recover.'

'Yes, yes, you are probably right. We've not been short of offers. Lord Falmouth and Lord James have both invited us to stay. We didn't want to make any decisions until after today though. William Junior was our priority.'

'Well, that does sound like the right thing to do. We've done what we had to do now though. We've given William Junior the respect he deserves and he is at peace now. I think you need to take one of these people up on their kind offers. Would you like Molly and I to make all the arrangements?'

Helen nodded and then glanced over at Fred. Her husband was deep in conversation with Mat, but she could tell by the faraway look in his eyes, he wasn't taking a single word in.

Emma followed her daughter-in-law's gaze.

'Don't worry, I will sort out Freddie. He's no use here at the moment. I am sure Mr Dawson knows that. A little break would do you both the world of good.'

Bit by bit, Helen and Fred allowed themselves to be helped out of Falmouth House. It was decided they would take up Lord James' offer first and then, possibly, spend a few days with Lord Falmouth on their way home. Emma said she would accompany them, to help Helen and keep a watchful eye on her son.

'You'll just need to keep things going smoothly at the hotel,' she told her husband. 'It won't be for long. Fred and Helen are the priority now.'

William Archer grumbled under his breath, but didn't question his wife. Part of him wanted to say Fred would be far better getting right back into racing to keep his mind off his personal tragedy, but something had changed in him since the death of his youngest son. Where once he would have said winning a race was the answer to everything, now he had his doubts. The expression Fred had in his eyes at the funeral reminded him so much of the look his youngest son had had on the day he died. He'd said he hadn't wanted to race, but William Archer had insisted. He'd been wrong. So very, very wrong.

'Let 'em take as long as they need,' William said, at last. 'You can trust me to keep things on track.'

Emma smiled at her husband. She knew how difficult this was for him too. Losing a child gives you a sadness you can never, ever shake off.

The following day, the small party made their way to Lord James' home in silence. Emma tried to make conversation as the train rattled its way through the countryside, but Helen and Fred said very little in return. The pair sat staring ahead into the distance, their hands still tightly entwined.

When they arrived at Lord James', an imposing Bath-stone mansion set in secluded gardens with stunning views of the valley around it, Helen and Fred seemed to brighten a little. It was as if the pair had unconsciously agreed they would start their healing process here, although neither had articulated this fact.

Lord James was outside to greet them, standing on the steps beside the stone pillars that marked the large entrance to his home.

'Welcome, welcome,' he said, helping first Helen and then Emma down from the carriage that he had sent to collect them from the station. 'I am so glad you all agreed to join me.'

Fred jumped down beside the women and Lord James shook his hand warmly.

'Thank you for inviting us, sir,' said the jockey.

'As always, I am being utterly selfish,' smiled Lord James. 'I intend to make complete use of your expert services while you are here. First though, I shall feed you all. You look exhausted after your journey. I believe the cook has prepared a rather hearty winter soup, with a pile of vegetables and beef stock, and judging by the aromas that are coming out the kitchen, there is some fresh bread just out of the oven.'

'You spoil us,' Emma laughed. She always felt lighter of heart when she saw Lord James, even despite the solemnity of the current circumstances.

'It is my greatest pleasure,' beamed Lord James. 'May I lead you to the dining room, Mrs Archer? Don't worry about bags, I will have them taken to your rooms and unpacked. Fred, I do hope you will be eating at least something with us?'

'I will, sir. I will.'

'Excellent, excellent. Come this way.'

After a delicious lunch, Lord James, Fred, and Emma retired to the drawing room for tea, while Helen went to lie down. She still felt easily exhausted after the trials of the birth and needed regular naps to keep her strength up.

'Is Helen recovering well?' Lord James enquired of Fred, after they had settled into chairs which were placed closely around the roaring fire.

'Yes, I believe so. Physically, anyhow. I think it will take a while to come to terms with losing our child.'

'It will do, Freddie,' soothed his mother. 'But you have each other. You are young and strong and there will be others.'

Fred looked down at the floor.

'I wish I had your strength of conviction,' he said quietly. 'I sometimes wonder if this family is cursed.'

Emma drew a sharp breath and glanced at Lord James. He was staring at Fred.

'Cursed?' Lord James said. 'Surely you don't believe all that superstitious nonsense. Honestly, this nation is obsessed with ghosts and ghouls and curses. It's all I ever read about in the newspapers.' Emma frowned and looked from one man to another.

'What do you mean cursed?' she prompted her son.

Fred sighed. It was difficult for him and he was conscious his mother had had her share of tragedy in recent years.

'I didn't say anything at the time, but Joe and I saw a fortune teller a few years back,' he began, speaking deliberately. 'I don't know why we did it. I thought it would be a bit of a laugh. I have never been superstitious. To be honest, I thought it was all a bit of nonsense.'

'And what did she say? That you'd win a lot of horse races?' Lord James chuckled.

'Well no, she didn't,' said Fred, refusing to rise to the bait. 'What she actually said was death and sadness was coming to me.'

The room was silent, bar the crackle of the fire and distant sounds of clattering in the kitchen. Emma glanced nervously at Lord James, who looked deadly serious now.

'A few months later, we lost William Junior in that dreadful riding accident.'

Fred's face was ashen as he said this. It was Emma's turn to look down. Tears fell down her cheeks.

'I hoped that was it. That everything was done. I was so happy after the wedding, I convinced myself I'd had the death and sadness and we could move on. Then we lost our own little William Junior. I do feel like we are cursed.'

The silence returned.

'But why would you be cursed?' asked Lord James gently. 'That doesn't make sense.'

'I know. It doesn't. You are right.'

'I believe we all make our own luck,' said the older man. 'You have had a tremendous career and have been very successful in everything you do. I firmly believe you need to focus on that now and forget all about curses and gypsies. When the time is right, you will have another child and will realise all these notions about fortunes being blighted is just nonsense.' Fred nodded, but neither he nor Emma looked convinced.

Sensing he wouldn't convince either of his companions, at least not for now, Lord James skilfully steered the conversation on to more general topics. Fred immediately seemed relieved and not a little grateful. He felt uncomfortable and foolish voicing his fears, even though he also felt compelled to mention them. Now, he brightened considerably as his friend asked his opinion on which horses he favoured for the coming season. The pair began to talk animatedly about racing, hardly noticing that Emma had not said a word for some time.

At long last Fred checked his pocket watch and said he would go upstairs to check if Helen was all right.

'If she feels up to it, perhaps we could take a turn around the garden before it gets dark?' suggested Lord James. 'It doesn't look its best at this time of year, because there are far too many leaves on the ground, but I have a few plants of which I am particularly proud.'

'That sounds like a lovely idea,' Fred agreed. 'I'd like some fresh air.'

He left the room, shutting the door behind him quietly.

Emma stared at the fire.

'Do you really believe what you said, Edward?' she said quietly.

'Believe what?' he replied.

'That you don't believe in curses.'

'No, I don't believe in curses.'

Emma looked thoughtful.

'But you clearly do, Emma, my love. What is on your mind?'

'You know what is on my mind. Ever since we, since I, since you know what happened between us, nothing has gone right.'

'You can't say that. I won't let you. I know it should be the biggest regret of my life, but it isn't. You know how I feel about you Emma. I love you with all my heart and always have. If things could have been different and you were not already betrothed to William, you would have been here with me forever.'

'Don't,' Emma said, blushing. 'You can't say that.

You can't even think it. Look what it is doing to us. I truly believe my family and I are being punished for my misdeeds. I feel utterly wretched that there is a possibility that Freddie is going through this because of what happened between us.'

'There is no such thing as curses. What Fred is going through now is just sheer, awful bad luck. It is dreadful, but it has happened and we have to help him, and Helen, deal with it. All this talk of curses and fortune tellers is just making it worse. We need to help them both focus on the future, but the real future, not some made-up mumbo jumbo.'

Emma looked over at Lord James and smiled. She knew he was being harsh on her on purpose, to help tear her away from her negative thoughts.

'You're right and Freddie did seem a lot brighter when you mentioned going out this afternoon.'

'Indeed he did. We have magic air here, you know. It brings a spring to your step. I have it pumped in especially.'

'And I thought you said you didn't believe in mumbo jumbo! Magic air indeed.'

'Ah, you've got me. You always were a fiendishly clever young lady. Now, let's get ready for that walk. Are you dressed warmly enough? There can be a chilling wind this time of year.'

They heard some low chatter in the hallway outside and in a moment they were joined by Helen and Fred. Helen looked a lot better after her nap and the married couple seemed more happy and relaxed. As Emma looked at them she mused whether there was, indeed, some magic air at Lord James' house. It certainly seemed to be helping her son and his wife.

Lord James' guests stayed for two weeks and then made their way back to their respective homes: Emma back to the hotel and the young couple back to Falmouth. Everyone was refreshed and greatly rested.

Molly was gratified to see Helen and Fred seemed much more like their old selves. They'd barely walked through the door before Fred had decided to get out to the stables to check on things and Helen was taking charge of the household. This Molly took to be a very good sign.

Molly's sense of the uplift in emotion was quickly proved right. Fred returned to racing with gusto. His first ride was in France at the Grand Prix de Paris, where he was engaged to ride St Blaise, the horse that had beaten him in the controversial derby. The French jockeys did their best to see off the English upstart and poor Fred was tied up in the scrimmage for much of the race, but managed to come a respectable second in a close finish. It was not the win he desired, but it was a satisfying sign of his return to form. His next race, the Prince of Wales's Stakes at Ascot, produced a clear win on Galliard, ahead of a worthy rival called Ossian. In the same week, Fred won the St James' Palace Stakes and the Triennial Stakes, again on Galliard.

Sadly for Fred, the revival of his fortunes did coincide with the end of one of the most successful pairings on the track. Lord Falmouth decided to retire and to dispose of his magnificent string of horses. The decision cast a gloom over the Heath House stable, after working with Lord Falmouth's horses for so long, but Mat and Fred did their best to make the most of it. The pair commissioned a silver salver and inscribed it with the names and dates of all Lord Falmouth's Classic winners. There were fourteen names in all, and all but two had been ridden by Fred. The inscription read:

'Offered for the acceptance of the Right Honourable Viscount Falmouth by his trainer and jockey Mathew Dawson and Frederick J Archer, as a token of gratitude and esteem to the best, kindest and most generous of masters on his retirement from the Turf, January 1884.'

While the loss of Lord Falmouth's patronage was a blow, this was not the only challenge for Fred to overcome. More pressing were a fresh set of rumours that began to beset the close-knit racing community. There were whispers about a 'jockey's ring' being operated, where certain unscrupulous riders were conspiring to fix races. People pointed the finger, saying only the horses chosen by the leaders of this ring would win, so if you weren't in the know, you would be at a real disadvantage. And who were the names alleged to be at the centre of this ring? None other than Fred Archer and another jockey called Charles Wood.

Fred was, of course, appalled when he first got wind of the rumours, which he knew to be utterly without foundation. Certainly in his case anyhow. He went straight to see Mat, clutching a notice that had been received by the Jockey Club.

'Have you seen this?' Fred said. 'Well meaning "friends" have been pointing me towards it all day.'

He handed the notice over to Mat, who read it out loud.

'To ask the stewards whether they are aware that it is openly stated that a conspiracy exists between certain jockeys and so-called "professional backers" of horses to arrange the result of races for their own benefit, and, if they have heard of such statements, and believe it is possible such a plot exists, what steps they propose taking to deal.'

Mat looked at Fred quizzically.

Fred sighed and shook his head.

'I heard a few rumours over the past few weeks, but I tried to ignore them,' he said. 'There are always people trying to throw stones ever since that derby. It's taken some time to make any sense of them, but some folk are saying the "certain jockeys" mentioned here are me and Wood.'

'I've heard something to that effect,' Mat shrugged. 'I've told everyone that has mentioned it that it is complete nonsense. How did it end up with this notice?'

'That is the crazy thing. It's from Sir George Chetwynd. He's gone off demanding all sorts of investigations and enquiries and, as far as I have been able to find out, the Jockey Club and stewards don't know a thing about it.'

'This would be the same Sir George Chetwynd that employs one Charles Wood, jockey of this parish?' Mat said slowly. 'He is basically calling for an investigation of his own man?'

'Exactly. It doesn't make any sense.'

'It looks to me as though he is using your name and reputation to act as a shield to protect Wood and, probably, himself.'

Fred looked at the ground and stamped his foot irritably.

'This is just what I don't need. More suspicion and yet again it is completely unfounded.'

Mat looked thoughtful.

'I will speak to some people and see what I can do to put an end to this. In the meantime, you need to do what you do best and get out there and ride some winners.'

Fred agreed this was the best course of action, although it was not easy to concentrate with the cloud of suspicion above him. He returned to the track, determined to prove his detractors wrong.

In reality, it took time for Fred to settle after the shock of the Jockey Club notice. He was defeated in the Two Thousand Guineas, then in the One Thousand Guineas and then in the Epsom Oaks. It was Helen that finally helped him to turn it all around.

She took him for a walk to their special place; the fallen oak where Fred had proposed what felt like a million years ago.

The pair settled into the well-worn seat in the tree.

'It is so beautiful here,' Helen breathed. 'It makes you believe anything is possible when you look upon a view like this.'

Fred nodded and squeezed his wife's hand.

'I am very proud of you, you know,' she continued. 'You have achieved so much and given us such a wonderful life.'

'It is me that should be proud of you and I am,'

Fred replied. 'None of this would be worth anything without you.'

'That is very kind, but I don't have to withstand all the nonsense from your so-called supporters that you do. I can't bear how these people try to knock you down all the time.'

Fred shrugged.

'It is the life I have chosen,' he said. 'I just need to rise above it.'

'Yes, yes, you do. I think you need to use their weakness and sniping as your strength. You must let it drive you on and not let yourself get distracted by all the dreadful things people say. What is your next ride?'

'I'm taking Melton to Ascot for Lord Hastings and the Duchess of Montrose has asked me to ride Energy and Corrie Roy for her too.'

'And what do you think of your chances?'

Fred laughed. He wondered what Helen was up to. She seemed to have a very determined line of questioning.

'Well, since you ask, I have always seen potential in young Melton. I will say, however, I am not entirely sure he is ready yet. The other two I feel quite confident about.'

'Excellent. I shall back you to win them all,' Helen smiled.

'Even though I know for a fact you are not the gambling type,' Fred grinned back.

'Well, I am afraid you have to win now,' Helen said with a small pout. Looking deeply into her husband's eyes she reached for his hand and placed it on her tummy. 'You've got to show our baby what a clever, talented daddy he has.' Fred's eyes widened.

'You are not…' he gasped.

'I most certainly am.'

'Oh, my darling, you clever, clever girl. Oh, my goodness. I can't believe it. How are you? Are you in good health? You don't feel too tired?'

Helen laughed.

'I'm absolutely fine. In fact, I feel wonderful and healthy and very, very happy.'

'But you need to rest. A lot. I will speak to Molly straight away and ask her to take on more duties in the house.'

'No you will not! I am perfectly capable of continuing a few light duties. Don't worry, I will take better care of myself. However, I am not retiring to bed for the next seven months.'

The pair walked back to Falmouth House, hand in hand, chatting excitedly about the future. Through a series of joking negotiations, Helen agreed that Emma and Emily could be asked to come and stay in the final few months of her confinement.

The news transformed Fred. Once more he had a real bounce in his step. He won all three of his Ascot races comfortably. He went on to win the Stewards Cup at Brighton, on a ride called Brag and the Yorkshire Oaks with Clochette. At the next meet in Thirsk, the Town Crier went through the streets proclaiming Fred Archer was 'The Wonder of the World!'.

By the end of the season, Fred had chalked up an impressive 200-plus winners.

The rumours about jockey circles did not go away though and it distressed Fred every time he caught the tail-end of a whispered comment. He'd often imagine people were discussing it, even when nothing could be further from the truth. There were still those that believed that, despite having more winners under his belt for the season than anyone else on the circuit, Fred Archer could be bought and persuaded to throw a race.

Luckily for Fred, he had a large group of loyal supporters, most notably the Duchess of Montrose. The Duchess would regularly invite Fred to her grand house at Sefton Lodge in Newmarket to deliver words of encouragement. It should be said though, Fred's association with the outspoken Duchess did encourage an entirely new set of rumours, since few jockeys could withstand her sharp tongue and ungovernable temper, despite the large retaining fees on offer. Fred was though, the perfect gentlemen. He was greatly experienced in gently letting down female admirers and he and the Duchess soon formed a strong bond, borne out of friendship and trust and a mutual obsession with the racetrack.

Over time, the Duchess became almost as much of a confidant as Freddie's beloved mother.

Fred happened to be at Sefton Lodge discussing the forthcoming season on the day he had received some worrying news.

'You seem somewhat distracted today, Freddie,' boomed the duchess. 'I do hope I am not boring you.'

'Not at all, I do apologise,' he countered quickly. 'I, I have just had a conversation I would rather not have had.'

'Well, what is it? Out with it. I am sure it can't be as bad as all that.'

Fred shifted in his chair uncomfortably. He really wasn't ready to discuss this matter. He had barely worked out what it meant in his own head.

'I met with Doctor Mitchell today. He is the one dealing with Helen. He asked to see me on my own.'

The Duchess put her cup and saucer down on the small table beside her and put her head to one side to indicate she was listening. Although a warm-hearted Irish woman, with a reputation of chattiness, the Duchess was also a good listener when she needed to be.

'He said he was concerned about Emma. It's not long since we lost William Junior. They are not sure what damage was done...'

His voice trailed off and he looked at the rich carpet beneath his highly polished boots. Again the Duchess held her tongue.

At last, choosing her words carefully, the Duchess said: 'I will admit Fred, I am very fond of you and, of course, Helen, and would do anything to ease your concerns. You must trust in the doctors though and listen to all the advice you are getting.

'You know you can always come to me. My door will always be open to you. Rest assured, I am your friend, as well, I might add, as a Duchess that likes her jockeys to be on top form at all times. You are not to worry needlessly, or it will take your mind off the job at hand. We can't have that, can we?'

'He thinks it might be a difficult confinement,' Fred said, the words tumbling out of his mouth in a rush. He could hardly bear to voice them.

'You men are not always right,' the Duchess said. Her voice was quieter than normal and noticeably more gentle. 'That is despite what you tell us ladies. Mistakes are made. I've never seen a stronger, more resourceful girl than your Helen. If anyone can withstand a difficult confinement, it is her.'

Fred nodded. His eyes were sad and scared.

'I can't lose her. I couldn't bear it.'

'Well, you can stop that sort of thinking for a start. That won't get you anywhere. Can you imagine what she would say if she heard you now? You need to be strong and positive. You need to be thinking like the winner you have always been.'

Fred dipped his head as a sign he understood. Deep down, he wasn't sure he agreed with the Duchess. Helen had tried to hide it from him, but she'd had a difficult pregnancy all the way through. Fred had done his best to convince himself everything was all right, wondering if his imagination was perhaps playing tricks because of what had happened with their first baby. There was no escaping the fact though that Helen was weak and tired. Often, when she didn't think Fred was looking, she would wince in pain.

They were just a few weeks away from Helen's due date now. Emma and Emily had taken up residence at Falmouth House and everyone was on tenterhooks waiting for the big event. Fred didn't like to leave the house at all, in case he was needed, but his mother and sister would regularly chase him away, telling him to go to work.

'You'll not do anyone any good, hanging around with a long face looking worried,' Emma said gently. 'We'll send for you if anything changes. Everything will be fine. You'll see.'

Fred wished he could believe his mother. He really did. The Archers really needed their luck to change, but Fred could not escape the feeling the odds were simply not in their favour this time.

CHAPTER NINE

Helen dreamily stretched her toes to the bottom of the bed and moved to turn to one side. For those few luxurious moments that lie between sleep and wakefulness she had forgotten the huge bump in her middle. The second she tried to shift her body to a more comfortable position though, she was abruptly reminded of it.

She also became aware she was not alone.

'You're doing it again,' she said quietly, with a low chuckle.

'Doing what?' Fred answered, pretending to be surprised by the statement.

'Sitting in that chair beside the bed, staring at me.'

'How do you even know that? Your eyes are still tight shut.'

Helen lifted her arm from beneath the covers and stretched her hand out towards her husband.

'Let me see. Firstly, I can always sense you when you are near me, my love. Secondly, you have been there most days when I awake, whether morning, noon, or evening.'

Fred laughed.

'I love being with you, you know that. I want to make sure you are all right too. If I am here at your side, I can react at any moment should you need me.'

'Ah, well, you have no worries there. I am being watched over day and night. If it is not your mother, it is Molly, if it is not Molly, it is Emily or one of my dear sisters, or my mother. Tell me honestly, do they have a rota written down somewhere?'

'I wouldn't discount that possibility at all, that is for sure. I don't blame them though. We all just worry about you and want you to be well.'

'I know, I know and I am so grateful to everyone. Everyone is being so kind. I do feel like I could scream in frustration though. I hate being stuck in this bed day and night with people asking me if I am well.'

Fred squeezed Helen's hand and then stood up and kissed her tenderly on the forehead.

'It won't be for much longer and in a few weeks' time you will look back and long for a good long lie in bed.'

Helen struggled to sit up and Fred stepped in to help her, propping cushions behind her until between them they managed to find a comfortable spot. Fred was careful not to articulate what he was thinking but it worried him how weak his wife had become.

'Now, sit down beside me and tell me about what is going on in the outside world,' Helen said, patting the bed to indicate where Fred should settle down. 'I don't want to talk about confinement, or health, or babies, or anything like that. What is happening about the Duke of Portland?' Fred settled onto the bed.

'Gosh, well that has turned into a bit of a saga. Where did I get to?'

'You told me about those silly rumours, the ones about George Alexander Baird and said the good Duke was very cross. Then we got interrupted, so you had better begin at the beginning.'

'Ah yes, Abingdon Baird,' Fred nodded. 'I am glad you are keeping up. Now, as you know, our friend Baird is a little unconventional and despite having built up a rather respectable stable of good horses here in Newmarket, he hasn't exactly endeared himself to the Jockey Club, one way or another.'

'Didn't he get warned off the Turf for two years, a little while back?'

'Indeed he did. Clever girl. There was some controversy over the Hunters' Selling Flat Race, where he was disqualified and then there was an awful row with Lord Harrington afterwards.'

'Oh yes, I do remember this. Didn't Mr Baird say he mistook Lord Harrington for a farmer in the weighing room!'

'That's right. Obviously, that didn't go down terribly well, but, truth be told, I think the punishment handed down by the Jockey Club was a bit harsh. Abingdon Baird certainly felt that way, but there you go. There are plenty of people in the racing establishment that don't ever want to see him back.'

'But he wants to make a comeback?'

'Yes, and with yours truly, if you believe the rumours.'

'I am not quite sure how that would work,' said Helen, screwing her face up into a small frown of concentration. 'You are partnered with Mat Dawson.'

'Nor am I. All I have managed to glean is Mr Baird has come up with the idea that he and I set up some sort of joint racing establishment in Newmarket. He'd told everyone about it before he even mentioned it to me, which is what gave me to believe it wasn't really a serious proposition.'

'But he did come to you eventually. So, what did you say when he approached you?'

Fred scratched his chin thoughtfully.

'He was very charming about it and said all sorts of complementary things, but I told him it was out of the question. I've got too much going on here.'

'Was Mr Dawson all right about it? He must have heard the rumours too?'

'Oh yes. He'd heard, but we had a talk about what was being said and he knows I am very happy with the partnership as it is. Mat Dawson gave me my start and I am not about to turn my back on him now.'

Helen smiled. She fully approved of Fred's loyalty.

'But the Duke of Portland was not so understanding?' she prompted.

'No, he was not. He sent for me and I went to his estate at Clumber Park, in North Nottinghamshire last week, as you know.'

'What did he say?' Helen said, her eyes wide in

anticipation.

'Well, I have never really seen him so angry. As you are aware, he has been a patron of Heath House since before I joined the stables for my apprenticeship and he has been a constant and generous presence. The Duke said that he had heard the rumours and strongly objected to any jockey of his coming to an arrangement with a fellow like Abingdon Baird.'

'Didn't he even ask you if the rumours were true first?'

'No, he didn't. It was what he said next that upset me the most though.'

Helen shifted in the bed uncomfortably and Fred paused his story to help her to a more satisfactory position.

'Can I get you some more water?' he said, looking concerned.

'No, no, I am fine. Please, please, do continue.'

Fred stared past Helen and out of the window at the other side of the room. It was as though he was struggling to say what happened next.

'He said that if I had decided to come to such an arrangement with Abingdon Baird, I should immediately sever it, or cease to ride in the Portland colours.'

'He threatened you?'

'I suppose he did.'

Helen was silent for a moment, taking it all in.

'If I was being kind I might say I could see it from his point of view. I was speaking with Mr Dawson afterwards and we agreed this was all tied up with the Duke's political life. He's not long been sworn into the Privy Council, so he obviously wants to be seen as whiter than white. He's also to be made Master of the Horse this year. He definitely does not want to have any association, even a third party one, with someone who is not of good standing.'

'But none of this means he couldn't have put this all a bit more diplomatically, does it?' Helen said. 'Those are pretty strong words, threatening to withdraw from Heath House.'

Fred shrugged. He looked resigned to it all.

'It's the world we live in,' he said at last. 'The Duke of Portland is the pillar of the ruling few and one of the richest men on the Turf.'

'So, what did you say?'

Fred sighed.

'I was quite angry when he said this to me, but I told him I would give the matter some consideration. On the train on the way back though, I became even more cross. I felt that after all this time and all the winners I have ridden for that man, he should have given me the benefit of the doubt. He should have seen that I am loyal and always have been. He had no reason to pre-judge me.'

Helen stayed silent. She could sense Fred was finding it difficult to articulate the last part of the story. It was still very raw.

'When I came home, I wrote the Duke a letter. Rightly or wrongly, I told him in terms that were as blunt as the ones he used with me, that I reserved the right to choose whomsoever I wanted as a friend or colleague, without fear of interference from anyone, no matter how highly placed in society.

'I also returned my cap and jacket in the Portland colours to the Duke, along with the balance of his retainer, which came to £400.'

Helen gasped and her hand flew to her mouth in shock.

'Oh my goodness,' she whispered. 'Was that wise? Surely he would have been furious. He is a powerful man.'

'That is true. You are, as always, completely right and extremely perceptive. You'll never guess what he did next.'

Helen stared at Fred, hardly daring to ask.

'What? What did he do?'

'He only went and leaned on Lord Hastings to encourage him to cut his ties with both myself and Heath House.'

'No, he can't do that!'

Fred looked alarmed at how animated Helen had become.

'Are you all right my love? If this story is getting you too upset, I shall not tell it any more.'

Helen looked at her husband reproachfully.

'I thought we had a pact where my health would not be a subject of discussion? I was just a little startled, that is all. Please carry on. What did Lord Hastings do?'

'Well, it would have been a bit of a disaster for us if we lost Lord Hastings as well as the Duke of Portland. We are already dealing with the hole left behind by the good Lord Falmouth's retirement.'

'And?' Helen prompted.

Fred broke into a smile.

'Lord Hastings gave the Duke short shrift and is staying put.'

'Thank goodness,' Helen breathed.

'Well, to be entirely cynical, I think Lord Hastings knows exactly what side his bread is buttered. Not to blow my own trumpet or anything, but now Lord Falmouth and the Duke of Portland no longer have a claim on my services, he will be left with first claim.'

'And, of course, you have the undivided attention of the Duchess of Montrose too.'

'That is true,' said Fred with a smile.

Helen pouted.

'Honestly, the way that woman flirts with you and sends you gifts, I am sure I should be very cross. In fact, I am sure I have the right to be more cross than the redoubtable Duke of Portland, that is for sure.'

Fred leaned forward and kissed his wife tenderly.

'You have no worries on that score. I only have eyes for you.'

Just then, the door swung open and Emily hurried in, carrying a tray laden with tea and small delicacies.

'Freddie, you've been talking nineteen to the dozen in here,' she exclaimed. 'I could hear you from the corridor. Don't you know Helen needs her rest?'

Helen and Fred exchanged glances.

'I thought you were going to Liverpool today?' Emily went on. 'Mr Dawson told me you were due to ride in the Autumn Cup.'

'Well, I wasn't sure. I wanted to be here with Helen.'

This time the two women exchanged glances.

'I'll be fine Freddie,' Helen said quietly. 'I thought our other agreement was that you would carry on as normal?'

Emily walked up to the side of the bed and began straightening out the covers. She then set to work on the crumpled heap of pillows, plumping them with cool and practised efficiency.

'Honestly Freddie, your poor wife looks exhausted. She'll be much better off without you talking to her and keeping her from her rest.'

'That's not true,' Helen giggled. 'It has been lovely hearing about what Fred has been up to. I just can't wait to get up and about again and see him race.'

'That would be nice,' Emily agreed softly. 'We should make some plans for after you have had the baby. Let's organise a big family get together for the first race of the season.'

'Yes,' agreed Helen dreamily. 'Do you remember that meet at Bangor, where we first met, Freddie? It was such a lovely day.'

'Maid of Trent,' Fred nodded. 'I was on Maid of Trent.'

'Oh Freddie,' Helen laughed, 'I can't believe your memories all centre around which ride you had that day.'

They all laughed.

'I remember the day very well, aside from the good Maid of Trent,' Fred corrected himself. 'And aside from the fact I won and quite convincingly too.'

Helen raised her eyebrows at her husband's teasing.

'I recall meeting the most beautiful woman in the world, who gave me a reason for living and the life I always wanted,' he continued.

Helen and Fred stared at each other, both overcome with emotion. Emily stayed silent, her heart swollen with pride.

'Thank you,' Helen breathed.

'Thank you for what?' answered Fred, never once taking his eyes off Helen's face.

'For making me so very happy.'

They smiled at each other warmly.

'Right, you two lovebirds,' Emily broke in. 'This young lady needs her rest if she is to be up and about gallivanting around the country to see your races soon. Are you going to Liverpool or not?'

'I think you should,' Helen said.

Fred nodded.

'As long as you are going to be alright here?'

'I'm fine,' said Helen, giving a mock sigh. 'Who are you riding today?'

'Thebais for the Duchess.'

'Well, good luck my love. Make it another winner.'

'I will. For you.'

Fred stooped down to give his wife one more tender kiss before he left. As he closed the door behind him and heard his sister chiding Helen for not getting enough rest, he smiled. He couldn't wait to have his wife up and about again and by his side.

Just a short time in her presence always transformed Fred. He felt happy, light of step and optimistic for the future.

His positive mood did not abate on the train journey to Liverpool and he excitedly began to make plans for the year ahead. As he stepped down from his carriage, Fred took a deep breath. This is it, he thought. He'd won 240 races so far this year and there was just a fortnight of the flat season left. It was very likely he would achieve a record number of wins for the season. He knew today, more than ever before, exactly why he did it: for Helen. The one being that made everything in his life worthwhile.

If he had known what was happening at home, he would have turned around and headed back immediately. At Falmouth House, Helen had gone into labour an hour after Fred had left. Dr Mitchell had called to check on her though, and all seemed well. Helen was adamant that no word would be sent to her husband.

'He'll be home this evening,' she said stubbornly. 'He'd only pace about if he were here and get in such a state.'

'I agree,' Grace confirmed. 'The doctor is so pleased with you and says the heartbeat is fine. If everything continues at this rate he will have a very nice surprise when he gets home.'

Fred was oblivious to what was happening though and once he reached the track in good time he set about making his usual meticulous pre-race preparations. As always, he was sure to make time to stop and speak to the handful of shy, young jockeys that were brave enough to come up to speak with him. They always said they wanted his advice on this or that. In reality, they just wanted to get close to the famous jockey and to feel his presence. They were so in awe of him when they met him, they forgot what he said completely.

Thebais was a good ride and the pairing had been successful on a number of occasions. Fred patted his neck as they headed down to the start line and looked across at his competitors.

'We've got this,' he said to the horse quietly.

He'd planned the race well. There was an unusually wide range of weights on the course and Fred, who was carrying 8st 12lb, according to the pre-race weigh in, was in the middle of the range, which went from 9 stone to 40 lbs. A strategy of running out as fast as possible, in an attempt to exhaust the opposition, was not the option, so Fred left that to others. Instead he kept to his plan of staying steady, only putting on a show in the last part of the race. His late surge was judged to perfection and Thebais won comfortably by three-quarters of a length.

'For you, my love,' whispered Fred shortly after he thundered over the line. 'For you and our baby, because together we are winners.'

Fred was still smiling as he rode into the winner's enclosure and effortlessly dismounted.

'Nicely done,' nodded Mat, taking Thebais' reins and patting him. 'Win number 241 and you didn't even break into a sweat.'

Fred laughed as he busily undid his saddle, deftly pulling the straps this way and that, as he had done a thousand times before. The leather creaked as it gave in to his well-practised routine.

'And nice to see you looking so happy too,' Mat added.

'I've got a lot to be happy about,' Fred called over his shoulder as he began to walk purposefully towards the weighing room, the saddle slung over his shoulder.

There were a number of formalities to be taken after the obligatory weighing-out that followed each race, but Fred wanted to keep moving. The quicker he got through, the quicker he could get back to Falmouth House to be at his wife's side if she needed him.

The steward greeted him by name the moment he walked through the door.

'I've got something for you, Mr Archer,' he said, darting behind a desk which was strewn with paper and pens. 'It's a telegram. Arrived when you were out on the course.'

Fred's heart skipped a beat and he felt a little weak behind the knees.

'Now, where was it?' the steward said, sounding a little bemused. He was pushing paper back and forth on the chaotic desk. 'I could swear I put it here. Oh no, now I remember, I put it in my jacket pocket for safe keeping.'

With a triumphant flourish, the steward produced a small rectangle of white paper from his pocket. Fred's mouth felt dry. He reached out to take it and the steward reached forward to help him put his saddle down on the nearby table top.

Using his index finger, Fred quickly tore open the telegram and read it.

'Congratulations on daughter stop Mother and baby fine stop'

Fred stared at the message and read the handful of words over and over again. Helen, his beautiful, clever, wonderful wife had had their baby. A little girl. Tears pricked at the corner of his eyes. He felt utterly overwhelmed.

'Is everything OK, sir?' the steward asked, looking concerned.

'Yes, yes, it is,' Fred nodded. 'I am a father.'

'Well, congratulations young man. That is fantastic news indeed.'

Fred was feeling a little dazed now.

'Shall we get you weighed?'

'Yes, thank you,' Fred said, mechanically picking up his saddle and heading towards the large scales. It was all such a shock. He'd only been talking to Helen a short while before and she had seemed so calm. After all that had happened last time, he felt sure he would have just sensed that she was about to go into labour. What an incredible woman she was, thought Fred. Truly remarkable.

'You done, Fred?'

It was Mat. He'd popped his head around the door to check on his business partner.

'You've been in here for ages. I just wanted to check you were alright.' Fred nodded and held out the telegram for Mat to see.

'She's had the baby,' he said quietly. 'She's feeling fine and the child is good too.'

Mat handed the telegram back and shook his friend warmly by the hand.

'Congratulations,' he smiled. 'Congratulations to you both. I couldn't be happier for you.'

'I need to get back to Falmouth House,' Fred said. Now the news had begun to sink in, he was unable to stop smiling. It was a deep, broad smile that lit up his whole face.

'Indeed you do. Right, well, we have the normal winner's shenanigans to go through here, but I reckon we can get you back to the train within an hour or so. Most importantly, I think we need a little celebration before you go anywhere, my friend. I hope you are going to join us to wet the baby's head in time honoured fashion.'

'That sounds like an excellent plan,' said Fred, still smiling from ear to ear.

Fred was desperate to start for home, but he wasn't about to abandon his winner's duties. He was too much of a professional for that. Besides, after waiting so long to be a father, he did agree it warranted a little bit of a celebration.

Word soon got around the track that Fred Archer

was a new father and crowds clamoured around the well-known jockey to offer their good wishes. His hand was shaken so many times and with such vigour his arm ached. Drink after drink was pushed his way and if he had supped them all he would have had great difficulty in boarding the train home with any degree of safety at all. Finally, with the night beginning to draw in, he managed to escape the racetrack and head off to the station. It was very late indeed when he finally arrived back at Falmouth House.

His mother was waiting up for him in the drawing room.

'Is everything all right,' he said, greeting Emma with a warm embrace. 'I am so sorry I wasn't here sooner.'

Emma smiled at her son. He looked pale and exhausted, but his beautiful eyes shone with happiness. He was such a handsome young man.

'Everything is fine,' she said, reassuringly. 'Helen is resting. She is very tired, but everything went as expected. In fact, better than expected. The doctor and midwife are very proud of her.'

'And our daughter?'

'She is beautiful. She has your lovely dark eyes and Helen's sweet face. She is quite perfect.'

'Where is she?'

'She is in her crib in the nursery. She's not long had her feed and the nurse has got her to sleep. I don't think anyone will thank you if you wake her now. Helen is awake though, and waiting for you.'

Fred embraced his mother again and hurried off to

see his wife. When he reached her room, he gasped. She was lying in bed and although she looked pale and tired, she looked more beautiful than he had ever seen her look before.

'Congratulations, my love,' he said, rushing to her side. 'You are the most remarkable woman in every way.'

'Have you seen her?' Helen murmured. 'She is beautiful.'

'I was told not to go in because she is sleeping. I couldn't resist a peek into the nursery though and yes, she is the most angelic creature I ever did see. Perfect in every way.'

Fred bent down and kissed his wife tenderly.

'Thank you for making me the happiest man in the world.'

Helen smiled.

'And thank you for making me the happiest woman. What is her name to be?'

Fred looked thoughtful.

'You mentioned Nellie Rose when you were pregnant. Do you still think that should be her name?'

'Yes, yes, I do. I would love that. Only if you are happy with it too, Freddie.'

'I couldn't be happier. In fact, I don't care what anyone says, I am going to go and see our Nellie Rose right now. It is high time she met her father.'

Helen laughed softly.

'You'll get into terrible trouble with the nurse,' she

whispered.

'I don't care. I could take on the world with my wife and daughter at my side. Now get some rest: I have so many plans for you and the lovely Nellie Rose.'

Helen closed her eyes and drifted off to sleep.

The following morning, Fred was awake early and got dressed into his hunting clothes. He wasn't entirely sure why he did this. He had it at the back of his mind that he might go out and hunt on the Drag, but part of him also remembered his wife had often said he looked best in his hunting clothes and he wanted to do everything he could to give her as much pleasure as she gave him. After checking his reflection in the mirror, he bounded out of his room. Emma met him in the corridor and said Helen was still sleeping, but his daughter was very much awake.

'Why don't you go to see her first?'

Fred headed eagerly to the nursery and flung open the door, his eyes searching eagerly for the crib. When he spotted it though, it was empty. It was only then that he noticed the nurse in her long grey uniform. Tucked into her arms was a small bundle of white lace.

The nurse looked up and gave a serene smile, beckoning him over with a nod of her head. Gently, she reached up, pulling the lace away from the top of the bundle to reveal a tiny, but perfect little pink face.

Fred gasped. She was faultless, like a tiny doll.

'She's a pretty one,' whispered the nurse. 'And a sleepy one too. You'll get no trouble from this little one.'

Fred reached out and gently stroked the baby's cheek. Her skin was unbelievably soft to the touch.

'Beautiful,' he breathed.

He stared at his daughter and felt a surge of pride. He did not think it was possible to be this happy and fulfilled.

After a while, Fred left the nursery quietly, impatient to see Helen at long last. He was desperate to check she was in good health, yet at the same time he didn't want to wake her if she was resting.

For a short while, he paced about the corridors of Falmouth, unsure what to do. He couldn't help noticing the house was unusually quiet. Perhaps, he reasoned, everyone was keeping the noise down so they didn't disturb the new arrival.

Suddenly, the silence was shattered by the most heart wrenching scream. It was a howl of pain the likes of which Fred had never heard. For a few seconds, he was rooted to the spot in shock. He knew that voice but today it sounded so different.

'Helen!' he shouted, breaking into a run in the direction of her bedroom.

His heart was pounding and his legs felt like there were lead weights attached to his feet. They simply wouldn't seem to move as he wanted them to. His breath was coming in short gasps and his throat felt tight.

'Helen,' he gasped again.

He was just a few metres away from the large white doorway, his eyes fixed manically on the goal. The door swung open abruptly and Molly ran out into the hallway. Her eyes wide and fearful as she looked up and down the corridor. As soon as she spotted Fred, she almost screamed. 'Fred, Fred, come quick. She's having convulsions. She, she…'

Fred didn't wait to hear any more, pushing past Molly and racing into the room. Grace followed close behind. They stopped short just a few steps in. The sight that greeted them was so shocking they were truly terrified.

Helen was in the most gruesome position. Her arms were flung wide and her back arched as she howled in agony. Her legs thrashed back and forth on the bed, which was completely bare of covers. Meanwhile, either side of her, Emma and a nurse were doing their best to hold his wife down to prevent her from injuring herself.

Stealing himself, Fred made the final few steps to the bed and caught hold of Helen's arms, as the nurse gratefully stepped to one side. He tried to help Helen down so she lay flat on the bed, but she fought back hard, her limbs thrashing around. Helen's eyes were wide and staring, but it was clear she had no idea of who was in the room with her.

'Helen, Helen, it's Freddie,' he shouted hopelessly. 'I'm here with you now. It is going to be fine.'

Emma stepped back now too and Fred glanced over with a look of agony on his face. The expression reflected back from his mother betrayed her complete shock and helplessness.

Abruptly, Helen's body stiffened and slumped back onto the bed. Her eyes were still wide, yet she saw nothing.

'Where is the doctor?' Freddie barked. 'Is he on his way?'

Emma nodded. Large tears were falling down her cheeks.

'What the hell is taking him?' Fred cursed.

Without warning, Helen let out a tremendous, heart wrenching howl. Her entire body arched at an angle of 90 degrees, her legs and arms stiffly below her. Then, just as abruptly, she slumped back in a crumpled heap without making another sound.

The room was completely silent. In complete desperation, Fred gathered Helen up in his arms. Her limbs hung limply by her sides. She was not breathing.

'She's gone,' whispered Emma, stepping forward and gently passing her hand over Helen's face to close her eyes. 'She's gone.'

'No, no, no,' Fred howled, burying his face into Helen, drinking in her familiar smell. She was still warm. How could she be dead?

'I'm so sorry,' Emma said, her cheeks wet with tears. 'She seemed so well and…'

Her voice trailed off. She really didn't know what to say.

Grace was sobbing loudly.

'My eldest has gone,' she wailed. She stepped forward and began pulling at the sheets, in a vain bid to make her comfortable. The room was silent as everyone felt the aching grief of a mother. Tears were falling from everyone's eyes.

Fred didn't move. He was holding Helen tightly,

like he would never ever let her go.

'What am I going to do now, Mother?' he murmured. 'What am I going to do now? How will I ever live without her? My life is over too.'

CHAPTER TEN

Those closest to Fred were doubtful he would ever recover from the shock and grief of losing his beloved Helen. He managed to hold himself together for the funeral, politely giving his time to the dozens of wellwishers who wanted to express their sadness at his loss. Afterwards though, he fell into a deep depression. He sat in the drawing room for hours at a time, simply staring into space, lost in a world of his own misery.

Emma watched over him like a hawk. She carefully policed the legions of people that called around to Falmouth House to pay their respects, only letting in a few of Fred's most trusted confidants a day. The others were politely asked to leave him be for now, but assured their kind wishes would be passed on. Even when people were shown into the drawing room, her son barely seemed to notice any visitor was there. Some days he would barely muster up the strength to say a word, despite the entreaties of those around him.

Most worryingly, he seemed to care little for his health and wellbeing. 'You've got to eat,' urged Emma gently. 'I haven't seen a thing pass your lips for days. I can almost see the weight dropping off you.'

Fred gave a rueful chuckle.

'Oh, the irony,' he said quietly. 'I spend my whole life starving and torturing myself to get to the right weight. For years, every waking moment, all I have thought about is how much I would like to eat properly, but I didn't dare because of my weight. I'd imagine all the foods I love most, how they'd taste and feel in my mouth, and how satisfying it would be to have a full belly. Now this happens and I would gladly never let a morsel pass my lips again.

'We should be grateful for small mercies, eh?' he concluded with a bitter laugh.

Emma sat down in the chair beside him and took both of his hands.

'Things will get better, my son. Not today, not tomorrow, but over time it will become easier. I promise you that.'

Fred stared ahead. He did not doubt his mother meant well, but he knew things would never be the same again. It didn't matter how hard time tried to heal.

'Little Nellie is well,' Emma said brightly, trying to bring things around to happier thoughts. 'Nurse says she is thriving. She's such a good little mite too. She's eating well and sleeping through the night all ready.'

Fred nodded, but didn't say anything. Part of him was desperate to spend time with his daughter, but there was a side of him that didn't dare go near her because she reminded him so much of Helen. It was all too raw. Too painful.

'Joe wanted to pop in to speak with you this morning,' Emma continued. 'I said that would be fine. I hope that is all right. There are a number of things to discuss about the yard, he said. Perhaps you should go out with him for a while and check over the stables?'

Fred shook his head. He had no wish to go out to look over the horses, or supervise the yard. He didn't see the point.

There were sounds outside in the corridor and then a soft knock on the door. Emma saw that Fred didn't move. He didn't even look up. Emma got up and went to the door to see who it was.

'Oh, good morning Joe, I was just speaking of you,' she said, standing back to let him through.

'Good morning, Mrs Archer, how are you today?'

'Very well, Joe. Do come through. Can I get some tea sent in?'

'No, no, I am fine thank you.'

Joe walked over to Fred who was slumped forward with his head in his hands. Every time he heard the greeting 'Mrs Archer' it cut him in two. Joe patted his shoulder.

'Morning Fred,' he said.

With a sigh, Fred slowly drew himself up and nodded at his friend by way of a greeting.

'I've come to ask you to rescue me,' Joe smiled.

Fred looked at him quizzically.

'How so?'

'I'm drowning under a sea of well-meaning friends asking me to convey messages to you. I can't get a thing done. I thought perhaps if you could come out and show your face I might be able to get on with my job.'

Fred gave the faintest of smiles.

'Don't worry my friend, they are coming at me from all sides here too,' he said quietly, waving his hand at a large pile of letters which were stacked on the table beside him.

'I've had notes from everyone, from the Prince of Wales, to the Duke of St Albans and all sorts besides.'

'They are just trying to be nice,' Emma broke in. 'It is very kind of them to take the time.'

Fred nodded and reached back to take one from the pile.

'There is even one from the Duke of Portland. It is a touch cold and impersonal after our run in over Abingdon Baird, but I suppose tragedy brings out the best in all of us.'

Emma and Joe didn't reply. Fred's humour had grown so dark lately, there was often no answer to his wry jokes.

'The note from the Duchess of Montrose was very kind and warm,' Emma said, valiantly doing her best to change the tone of the conversation. 'She seems very concerned over your welfare.'

Joe looked at Emma pointedly and raised an eyebrow. They both giggled.

'Well, yes, anyway, the point is, people are willing you to get back onto your feet,' Emma said, blushing slightly. 'She does have an interesting suggestion too. She thought you might go away on a trip.'

'It's not such a bad idea,' interjected Joe. 'A change is as good as a rest and all that.'

'She thought perhaps America would be good for you,' Emma continued. 'You've never been and there is no need to worry over the language. The Duchess says she has many friends and acquaintances there that she could introduce you to and some suggestions of where to stay.'

Fred was silent and contemplative.

'I could come with you,' Joe said tentatively. 'I've always wanted to go to America.'

'What about the yard?' Fred said.

Joe and Emma exchanged glances. Fred's question indicated he was considering the proposition. This was progress indeed.

Joe thought on his feet.

Speaking rapidly, lest Fred changed his mind, Joe said: 'Well, we've passed the end of the season now, so things are automatically a lot quieter. I'm sure Mr Dawson won't mind taking charge and I have a number of young men that are itching to take on more responsibility. This is the perfect opportunity to test them out.'

The room lapsed into silence while Fred mulled it over. At long last Fred spoke.

'All right then, I will go. Thank you Joe, I would like it very much if you would accompany me. I would be most grateful too if you would both help me in making the arrangements. I struggle a little with my concentration these days.'

'Of course,' Emma broke in. She was trying her hardest not to cry out of a mixture of relief that Fred was at last moving on a little, tempered by the fact her beloved son was about to head off to the other side of the world.

'There is something that I do have to do before I go anywhere though,' Fred said.

Emma and Joe looked at him expectantly.

'I would like to make a Last Will and Testament. This is a long trip and who knows what will happen. I want to be sure Little Nellie is provided for should anything happen.'

'Of course you do, my friend,' Joe said quickly. He had seen the look of shocked surprise on Emma's face and didn't want to lose the momentum of Fred's resolve. 'I reckon Mr Jessop should be able to help you there.' Mr Jessop was the solicitor used by Heath House for all of its transactions.

'Do you think he will deal with this sort of thing, Joe?' Fred asked.

'I'm sure he will. The law is the law isn't it? Do you want me to come to with you when you go to see him?'

'No, that is kind, but I will be fine on my own with Mr Jessop. Besides, if you are to come travelling with me, you will have a lot to sort out here first.'

'Well, that is all decided then,' Emma said, now fully recovered from the introduction of the idea of

Wills. 'If it is all right with you Freddie, I will send a note to the Duchess to thank her for her useful suggestion and to take her up on her kind offer of introductions.'

'Thank you Mother,' said Fred, rising from his chair. 'Although I may call on her on the way back from seeing Mr Jessop.'

Emma winced when she saw her son's gaunt frame. He looked terrible. She really hoped the change of air would help in his recovery.

'As you like,' Emma concurred. 'I shall send a note to say thank you in any event. I am so glad to see you with some purpose again.'

Fred hardly heard his mother say this as he headed towards the door. He was already going over a list of his bequests in his head.

Fred no longer feared death. Losing Helen had shown him that things could be snatched away at a moment's notice. While it was not easy to do so right now, he was beginning to wonder why he had never allowed himself to live each day as it came. Starving and purging himself, which played havoc with his mood, had dominated his life for too long. In the run-up to some races, where he had had to lose large amounts of weight, he had often been too exhausted and melancholy to speak to his wife and had regularly answered her entreaties with brief one- or two-word answers. He knew she must have been hurt and offended, but she understood his reasons and never said a word in reproach. Fred regretted his behaviour now. He had wasted what little time he had with the love of his life.

The big question and the one he had been grappling with for days, as he sat in his chair, was: how could he put it all right? It was too late now to make it up to Helen. The obvious answer was to give Little Nellie the life she deserved. The poor little mite would never know the beautiful, wonderful woman who brought her into this world and would be all the worse off for that. It was up to Fred to give her everything and see that she was well provided for.

In time, once the period of intense grieving was over, Fred would find a way to reconcile himself with his daughter. It was not his baby girl's fault she reminded him so strongly of Helen. He'd need to get over that and this trip was his first step in trying to do so. Fred reasoned that if he gave himself a little space, he would miss home and his child so much, it would help him get through the barriers to his affection towards her. In the meantime, he would ensure that Little Nellie was assured of a generous legacy should anything happen to him. Fred decided to leave the bulk of his fortune to his daughter, after making a generous provision to support his father and mother, and a number of small bequests to his loyal and trusted aides.

The Will was completed with great speed, despite Mr Jessop's grumbles about the paucity of the instructions and the pace at which Fred Archer wanted the work done. In addition to carefully listing his goods and chattels, Mr Jessops insisted that Fred nominated guardians for Little Nellie, should Fred pass away while the girl was still in a minority. Without hesitation, Fred nominated John and Grace Dawson. While Emma would have been the obvious choice, Fred wanted his daughter to grow up in and around the family home in Newmarket. That is where his heart was, for now and ever more.

With the Will signed, Fred, Joe, and a valet made their way by train to Liverpool and from there they sailed for America aboard the steam passenger ship *SS Bothnia* on November 15th, 1884. After a brief stop in Queenstown, Ireland, the *SS Bothnia* made the trans-Atlantic route in just five days, arriving in New York on November 20th.

As the large ship steamed into New York harbour, Fred stared in awe at the Statue of Liberty.

'It's pretty amazing, isn't it?' Joe said. As usual, he was never far away from his friend. 'It only opened last month. Took over nine years to construct.'

Fred nodded, but didn't say anything.

'It's big, eh? Mind you, I was speaking to the Captain last night and he said everything is bigger here in America. Ah, here he is now. Everything going all right Captain Bowling.'

Fred turned and smiled in greeting at the ship's Captain. He was a short, tubby man, who constantly looked as though he may burst out of his smart blue uniform. The fabric around his bronze buttons certainly looked pretty taut. The pair had discovered very early on, that the Captain was a huge racing fan and he had spent much of the voyage doing his best to stay in close proximity to Fred.

'All is fine, thank you Joe. I have received a wire though and I think you had better both prepare yourself.'

'How so?' enquired Fred, looking concerned.

'Oh, no, it is nothing untoward, it is just there is quite a bit of press interest here about your visit. I have received requests from a number of reporters to pay their respects once we berth.'

Fred and Joe glanced at each other. This was the last thing they expected. Fred could hardly imagine they had ever even heard of him on the other side of the Atlantic.

'I see,' the jockey said at last. 'I had hoped this trip would be rather low key. I'm certainly not here on business.'

'They'll be fine with that Mr Archer. I've seen this happen a lot. They are always interested to talk to a well-known name coming this way. If I could be as bold as to give you some advice?'

'Of course, please do.'

'Give them some time now and tell them what you just told me, that you are not here on business and simply want a break. That way, they'll get what they came for and they'll leave you alone after that.'

'That sounds reasonable,' Joe said, looking over at Fred. 'What do you think?'

Fred shrugged.

'Fine with me I suppose.'

'I'll warn you now, they can seem an intimidating lot,' the Captain offered, by way of further advice. 'I had a stage actress on board not long ago, Florence Farr, perhaps you have heard of her? The reporters went crazy for her.'

Fred looked alarmed and Joe shot the Captain a warning look.

'Their bark is a lot worse than their bite,' the Captain said hurriedly. 'If you speak to them nicely, they will give you an easy time of it. They seem to hate it when people put on airs and graces and when they do, they spend a lot of time trying to shoot them down. Tell them how much you like America, or how you are looking forward to spending time here, and you'll have made friends for life.'

Joe looked at Fred, searching his face for signs of disquiet.

'I'm sure it will be fine,' Fred said. Then he added generously: 'Particularly now the good Captain has given us such a fulsome briefing.'

The Captain beamed, delighted to have been of service to his hero. He then hurried off to oversee the berthing in New York.

Fred and Joe peered over the side of the steam ship as crewmen ran about pulling on ropes and sorting out bridges and walkways. The Englishmen immediately spotted the group of reporters. Their garb was unmistakable. They all wore virtually matching long brown coats, with highly polished brogues peeking out from below the hems. Each had a bowler hat, pulled low over their ears in vain protection against the biting wind that blew through New York harbour.

'Let the fun begin,' Fred said dryly as he saw them move en masse towards the gangplank.

Despite the Captain's warnings, the reporters were a friendly enough bunch. It probably helped that they immediately warmed to the serious, quietly spoken English jockey. They certainly seemed to appreciate his quick witted answers. Most of their questions were pretty predictable.

'Are you planning to race while you are here in America, sir?'

'Which one was your most sensational victory?'

'Do you have a favourite ride?'

'What is your tip for the next season?'

As was his custom, Fred gave detailed and thoughtful answers. He knew his horses so well and could list their strengths and weaknesses without missing a beat. The reporters scribbled away in their notebooks, nodding in appreciation and jostling with one another to get the next question in. Fred was undoubtedly off to a good start.

When the newsmen had finally exhausted all their questions, the Captain, who had been hanging around in the background with an anxious expression, ushered them off the ship and moved to help Fred and his party disembark.

'Thank you very much for all your help,' Fred said, stopping to shake Captain Bowling warmly by the hand.

Joe noticed with pleasure that Fred was smiling. It was the first time he had seen a genuine smile from his friend for a long time. He hoped this was the start of what he knew would be a long process of him returning to his former self, if indeed this were ever possible.

'Come on,' Joe said, once they had got down the

gangplank. 'First stop, Fifth Avenue. We're staying at the Brunswick Hotel and are due to dine with General Vanderbilt this evening.'

'General Vanderbilt?' Fred asked, looking at his friend with faint amusement. He'd never heard of the General, let alone ever met him before. 'I hope I will be glad I have listened to you on all these fine folk we are going to be staying with.'

'Ah yes,' confirmed Joe. 'This is the first of many engagements, courtesy of the good Duchess. You are to be fêted by New York's finest, my friend. Put an extra notch in that belt of yours, because you are going to be fed and watered like never before.'

'Then it is a good thing I have no intention of racing while I am here,' Fred smiled.

'Indeed it is,' confirmed Joe. 'You are a tourist, on your holiday. It is time to relax and see the sights.'

Fred didn't argue. The chance to forget his former life, at least for a short while, was an enticing process. Then, perhaps if he were not permanently in pain, his recovery could truly begin.

The visit to New York was the first leg of an exhausting tour which was to last nearly four months. After New York, which was richly caked in a thick layer of snow with the mercury stuck at a very chilly minus two degrees, Fred and Joe headed south. Their destination, New Orleans, was a comparatively balmy fifteen degrees in comparison. While Fred welcomed the rise in temperature, he didn't much care for the party culture of the French Quarter in New Orleans. Indeed, he found the constant noise of singing and music playing an assault on his senses. He was relieved that the next part of the tour was to head off into the wilds of Louisiana for a lengthy shooting trip. This was much more his sort of thing and he and Joe immediately agreed to extend the length of time they spent there.

Joe and Fred loved the rich vegetation of the bayous and Fred, in particular, was fascinated by the diverse range of wildlife there. The first time he came across an alligator resting on the bank, he nearly shouted in shock, but was strangely drawn to the creatures. Perhaps he saw a kindred spirit in them. Far from being slow and detached, as everyone often said they were, Fred saw a being that would painstakingly plot its strategy as it carefully observed the world around itself. Then, when the time was right, they would move like a lightning bolt towards their goal, timing their hunt to perfection. Fred respected that.

After they emerged from the wilds of Louisiana, Fred and Joe headed north once more, taking in Washington and Chicago, before getting as far as Niagara to observe the renowned waterfalls which were a spectacular sight, like nothing either man had seen before. The pair then headed south again, visiting St Louis, Houston and Texas, before returning to New York in early March.

Joe kept in constant touch with Emma, just as he had promised to do, and was pleased to inform her that her son seemed to be in much finer form. He illustrated a recent event as a case in point in one of his letters.

'Fred is pursued by people everywhere he goes, just as he is back at home,' he wrote to Emma. *'I never knew Americans knew so much about our racing. Even celebrities*

flock to meet him and vie to secure his presence at their soirees. I've never seen such sumptuous feasts either. I am sure I have doubled in size since we have been here. Fred too.'

Emma smiled to herself as she read the letter. She was sure Joe was exaggerating, but the fact that Fred was eating even half way normally was a huge relief.

'The strangest thing happened today,' Emma read on. 'Fred was invited to visit a most notorious prisoner who is being held in the Tombs, here in New York. The Tombs is their big prison here. He was invited to see a lady by the name of Yseult Dudley. You may have heard of her? She was the Englishwoman who took the liberty of asking to meet with so-called Dynamite O'Donovan as a potential donor. If you haven't read about him in the papers, he was expelled from England after a spell in prison for all sorts of bad behaviour connected with Irish resistance to British rule. Anyway, Miss Dudley was quite cross about it, by all accounts, so she shot him! Several times too.

'Your Freddie was rather taken with her and the two of them had a very cosy chat. She told him she intended to come to England and shoot Mr Gladstone next. Do you know what Fred said afterwards? He said she was one of the finest women he ever saw!

'I thought you might like to know this. While Miss Dudley is probably not suitable material for a new daughter-in-law, it is at least a good sign that your son's recovery is proceeding well.

'We are, as you know, heading back on SS Bothnia next week and we may well reach you before this letter does. If so, we will have already told you about our many adventures. If we are yet to arrive, fear not, there is much left to share with you.'

Emma smiled and carefully returned the letter into its envelope. It had, in fact, arrived the day before the travellers were due to dock in Liverpool and Emma's heart beat faster at the thought of her son returning.

As it was, the *SS Bothnia* was delayed thanks to bad weather during the crossing and Fred and Joe did not make it back into Liverpool until a day later than expected, on March 9th.

Fred hurried back to Falmouth House with a lot on his mind. The start of the new season was just days away and there was a lot to prepare. After the lengthy trip, he now knew something for certain; he could never turn his back on racing. Whatever else happened to him, this was his lifeblood. Although still consumed by grief, his mind was constantly on the track wherever he went in America. Despite all the extraordinary sights and sounds he experienced, he always reverted to equating them to the equine world, comparing everything with what happened on the track.

Emma ran down the hallway corridor like a schoolgirl the moment she heard the carriage bringing her son home. She'd stayed at Falmouth House on and off over the past four months, to make sure everything was kept on track and had been sure to be there for her beloved Freddie's return. Little Nellie had, in particular, stolen her heart and she loved to be there to help with the little girl's care.

She stood on the front steps, her hand clasped to her mouth in pride as Fred stepped down from the carriage.

'Freddie, you look so well,' she cried. 'Welcome home.'

'Well?' Fred chortled. 'Don't you mean I look so large? You won't believe how much I weigh now. Joe was right. Everything about America is large, including the meals. I am tipping the scales at 9 stone 10 pounds now. Joe says I will have to chop off at least one leg before I am allowed to race this season!'

Emma shook her head, laughing as she did so. Her son seemed so much better. She did hope it wasn't all bravado and that he truly felt healed inside. Only time would tell though.

'It is wonderful to see you, Mother,' Fred said, reaching to give his mother a hug.

Emma held Fred tightly. It was so wonderful to have him back where he belonged. Finally, she let him go.

'I have gifts,' Fred announced, nodding towards the bulging parcels which were precariously strapped to the back of the carriage. 'And one very special gift, for a very special young lady. Where is Little Nellie?'

'The nurse is just waking her now,' Emma said. 'We weren't entirely sure what time you would be here. What did you get for her? Nothing too extravagant, I hope. We don't want to spoil her.'

'You worry too much, Mother. It is a basketwork perambulator. They are all the rage in New York. All the rich ladies have them.'

'My, my, won't we look mighty fine from now on then,' Emma teased. 'Oh Freddie, it is so lovely to have you back with us.'

Fred took a step backwards and stared up at the house he had built for himself and Helen. Deep down he knew things would never be the same again and it was inevitable that this large house would feel empty and lonely. He owed it to Helen to go on, though. He also owed it to their young daughter.

At that moment a nurse appeared with Nellie Rose in her arms. Fred gasped. He honestly thought his heart would stop. She had grown so much in just four months and her shock of unruly golden hair looked just like Helen's.

'Come on, old man,' Joe said, giving him a playful slap on the back. 'You've got work to do.'

'You're right,' Fred agreed. 'I think my first port of call, after I have spent some time with Little Nellie here, should be to visit Mary Rose Dawson to fetch a vat of her special mash. I am not sure how long it will take me to shift all this weight, but I can't see myself eating anytime soon.'

'Oh Freddie, you still need to eat,' chided Emma, only half-jokingly. 'You've got to keep healthy.'

Emma knew her pleas were falling on deaf ears, but it felt strangely comforting to be returning to some resemblance of a routine. She'd had that conversation with Fred a hundred times or more. Fred, as always, dismissed her pleas with a shake of his head.

'Right,' shouted Fred. 'Give me that young lady. She needs a hug from her father.'

CHAPTER ELEVEN

Paradox, as the name would suggest, was a most extraordinary horse. He had a turn of speed like no other, yet he had a secret. It was a secret no owner would want the outside world to learn about, because it was a serious blight to his chances as a racehorse. Each time he got onto the track he'd quickly make his way to the front. However, the very second he saw daylight at the head of the pack, he would invariably drop his bit and cease to try.

There were few jockeys in the land with the strength and presence to persuade Paradox to run on at a time like this. Fred Archer was one of them.

It was fitting that Fred's return to the track should be with Paradox. The pairing, for the Two Thousand Guineas which was the first race of the season, seemed to echo Fred's own internal struggle on how to find his way.

There were high expectations for this race. The odds were 3-1 on for Paradox, but mainly because Paradox's peculiarities had been carefully hidden from the world at large. The bad news for Fred was his rival, Tom Cannon, who was paired with Crafton, was one of the handful of people who did know about Paradox's weakness. Like Fred, Tom was a skilled strategist on the track and he was not about to let opportunity as good as this pass.

When Fred set off for the Newmarket racetrack, Mat Dawson noticed with some satisfaction that his partner had something of the familiar hungry glint in his eye. He was very obviously utterly focussed on the race ahead and as determined as ever to prove his mettle. It had been a tough winter for the young jockey, but he had pushed himself harder than he had for some time. He had been out training in all weathers and was a near constant presence in the yard. Somehow, and Mat was never sure how, Fred had managed to lose an extraordinary amount of weight and was back down to just over 8 stone, which was no mean feat for a jockey who was so unusually tall.

'You shouldn't try to lose too much weight too quickly,' Mat warned. 'It's not good for you. You need your strength too.'

'Nonsense, it is exactly what I should do,' shot back Fred. 'Besides, being on the track takes my mind off the last six months and I know I will feel even better once I start winning again.'

Fred was indeed consumed by racing once more and not just this event either. In his mind, he wanted this to be his best season ever, with the most winners. Only then, perhaps, would the pain which constantly dogged him finally subside. In his heart of hearts, Fred was doubtful that the joy of victory could defeat his deeply held grief, but it was the only solution he could come up with which came near to sounding feasible.

As Fred mounted Paradox, he ran through the race in his head once again. He blocked out the noise of the crowd and stared ahead at the track breathing deeply, drinking in the comfortingly familiar smells of the track. He knew Cannon would try his hardest to keep Paradox out front for as long as he possibly (and safely) could. It was exactly what he would have done. His best option was to let this happen and to force his ride to keep up his legendary pace without buckling under the pressure.

When the starter called the race and set the riders off thundering down the track, Fred was proved entirely right. Cannon held Crafton back, so he was just behind Paradox. To begin with, this was fine, since Paradox was safely surrounded by the rest of the field, but the closer Paradox came to the front, the more his legs and shoulders began to stiffen. Fred felt the change in mood and judged his response to perfection. With the winning post in his sights he pushed Paradox on with a sharp crack of the whip. The horse could not refuse the experienced jockey, caught hold of the bit and stretched his neck forward. Cannon, who was a length behind, was caught by surprise as Paradox surged away. The other jockey knew he had left it too late for his run and cursed himself as he saw Fred cross the winning line comfortably ahead of him.

Fred Archer, the hero jockey everyone loved to love, was back and the crowd was delighted. The horses had barely started on their walk to the winner's enclosure when the crowd began to chatter excitedly about the big derby race in Epsom. The racing community was alive with speculation. Who would be engaged to ride which horse in the light of today's convincing win?

Mat caught up with Fred in the winner's enclosure and walked over to congratulate him.

'Well ridden, Fred,' he smiled, grabbing Paradox's reins and patting his neck. 'You seem to have got this one's measure.'

'She's an odd one all right,' Fred said, dismounting. 'I think I understand her manner now. Do we have any news on the derby?'

Fred was already starting to work on his saddle, ahead of the weighing. Mat couldn't help but notice how serious he looked. Fred certainly didn't seem like someone who had just won a big race.

'Yes, I've just been speaking to Lord Hastings,' Mat answered. 'He's exercising his retainer and would like you to ride Melton.'

Fred nodded.

'So who is going to take Paradox?' he said, looking at the horse in front of him. He looked around and then added quietly: 'If it is Cannon, we may have a problem. He knows about his "little problem" as well as I do. If he knows this one's way of running, he'll have the brains to think up a decent scheme to get him over the line, just as I did.'

Mat shrugged.

'I don't think anything has been decided yet, but the rumour is Lord Rosebury wants Cannon for one of his. I suspect Fred Webb might end up with Paradox.'

Fred looked thoughtful as he hoisted his saddle up on to his shoulder.

'Well, let me know if you hear anything,' he said, disappearing off in the direction of the weighing room.

Fred didn't want to admit it, but he was finding this first race meeting a real trial. He'd long struggled with the crowds and adoration and now he felt more isolated than ever. As soon as he was able, after completing the weighing and the post-race events, he quickly returned home to Falmouth House.

He was met at the door by Molly.

'I hear you did rather well today, young Fred,' she said, smiling broadly. 'You do make us proud.'

'Thank you Molly,' Fred said and smiled.

Inwardly Molly felt like her heart would break when she saw these faint smiles from her dear friend. He seemed so very far away from being himself. She wished there was something she could do, but knew the best thing was to carry on as normal and leave time to do the healing.

'While you were there, the Duchess of Montrose sent her messenger,' Molly said, handing Fred a note in a dainty, cream-white envelope. 'She has asked for you to call on her at your earliest convenience.'

Fred took the note. This was not an unusual event these days. Over the past few months the Duchess had sent him letters, invitations, and telegrams on an almost daily basis. She'd even sent him telegrams while he had been in America. Each one was more charming than the last. At first Fred had imagined that she had simply been looking out for her favoured jockey in his time of need, but now he realised it was a lot more than that. In fact, the Duchess was becoming quite ruthless in her pursuit of him.

For Fred, the attention was both flattering and confusing. Leaving aside the fact he had not long buried the love of his life, the Duchess was a lot older than him and from an entirely different social class. It was inconceivable that the two of them could become a legitimate partnership. It would be the biggest scandal to hit society for decades: the young widowed jockey from a working class background and the twice widowed Duchess.

At the same time, Fred was so very lonely now. He had no one to talk to, at least not in the way he used to speak to Helen. His wife had been so quick-witted, vivacious and perceptive. He had been able to discuss almost anything with her. Strangely, the Duchess had come closest in matching this interaction because she was intelligent and seemed to know so much about an extraordinary wide range of subjects. It was for this reason Fred so readily responded to the Duchess' invitations and became such a frequent visitor at Sefton Lodge.

As Fred returned to the stables to saddle up a horse for the journey over, he thought back to a conversation with Mat from a few weeks earlier.

He asked, nonchalantly, almost in passing: 'If I married the Duchess, would I become a Duke?'

Mat looked surprised for a moment and then let out a great gale of laughter.

'Don't be a damned fool,' he chuckled.

Fred blushed, but he knew his business partner was right. It was nonsense and entirely out of character to even think this way. He should do what he always did with the women who openly pursued him: enjoy their good company and be flattered by their attentions. He had no idea what he was thinking when he had voiced such a foolish notion to his partner and bitterly regretted having raised it at all. It must surely have been yet another symptom of how lost and lonely he was. He really was having some difficulty in thinking straight.

Fred arrived at Sefton Lodge in good time. He always loved the sweeping views of the estate from the entrance track. The lush green lawns were kept to near perfection by the large teams of groundsmen and the house itself was impressive to see. Indeed, it looked like a fairy-tale palace and seemed to stretch out in every direction, with the large York-stone patio that skirted each side giving the impression it was even larger than it was. There must have been at least a dozen large chimneys dotted over the roof, standing like imposing sentries guarding the fortress below. Everything about it spoke of luxury and elegance.

'What were you thinking, Fred Archer?' he asked himself as he dismounted and handed the reins to the young stable lad. 'Duke indeed. You're just a poor working-class boy, made good with the help of a lot of luck and a bit of talent.'

As the lad led his horse off, Fred glanced at the stables beyond. They were in pristine condition, with forty-five individual stalls, each with a smartly painted, glossy, split double door. The floor was swept to a pristine standard of cleanliness. Everything was on a grand and perfect scale. Fit for a King. Or a Duchess.

Fred shook his head at his own foolishness and walked to the front door. A footman greeted him and showed him through to the large hallway, where he was passed to a maid. The young woman in a spotless and highly starched black and white uniform showed him to the large, brightly lit and opulent drawing room and asked him to take a seat.

'The Duchess of Montrose will be with you shortly, sir,' she said, giving a small bob of a curtsy.

Fred smiled and nodded to acknowledge this. He felt comfortable enough here. God knows he had spent enough time at many noblemen's mansions. He never truly felt he fitted in though. In his heart of hearts, he was still the young boy who grew up in a village, crammed into the tiny backrooms of a public house, sharing a bed with his two brothers. His dear mother Emma had come from a good family and people said she had aristocratic airs, but nothing she could have taught him would have prepared him for this lifestyle. The only reason he was here now was because he had a God-given talent. No wonder he felt like an imposter.

'Ah, Freddie,' boomed a familiar voice. 'Fresh from your latest triumph. I can't believe you found time to come over to call on me. I am so grateful though.'

Fred leapt to his feet and took the hand that was held out to him. He bent low and brushed his lips lightly on the back, just as he had seen Lord James do with his mother dozens of times. No matter how often he did it though, he still always felt just a little bit awkward. There was certainly more than a trace of his father in him. He couldn't imagine William Archer managing to charm the nobility.

'Now, do sit down,' the Duchess ordered. 'I want to hear about that race from your point of view. I have heard about it from others, but I never believe a word until I have heard it from you. You are the only person I can trust to give me an honest account of the race.'

'You flatter me,' smiled Fred, settling into a chair.

'No I don't, it is quite true. Now come on. People say you are back to your old form and fully recovered. Well, are you?'

Fred wasn't quite sure how to answer this. He knew what society expected him to say. By convention, he had had his time of mourning. He should now be casting off the shackles of grief and resuming life as normal. He didn't feel this way though. Far from it. The win on Paradox had really brought it home to him. It had brought him no happiness at all. The question was, could he tell the Duchess this? Or, more importantly, should he?

Fred weighed it up in his mind, just as he weighed up a race. If he told her the truth about how unhappy he was, would she somehow be offended and stop her patronage of Heath House? That would certainly be disastrous for the yard. If she did accept it though, he would have someone in the world he could talk to, openly and frankly. He yearned for someone like this. If he couldn't have Helen, which he sadly couldn't, he might at least find happiness with someone like the

Duchess. Despite her somewhat forthright manner, she was very pleasant to spend time with and he did feel comfortable with her, even given the gulf in their backgrounds.

Finally, he made up his mind.

'To tell the truth, I found it a bit of a struggle today,' he admitted. 'I enjoyed the ride, but it is everything that goes with it that is hard to bear. The crowds, the Press, the backbiting. You know what the racetrack is like. There is no other place like it on earth.

'Every time I finish a race, I always have the same thought: Oh, Helen will be pleased with how that went. Or, I must tell Helen about such and such that happened. It is always a shock when I go home and realise she is not there. There is always my lovely Little Nellie and the house is full of other folk too, but it is not the same. It never is.

'I wonder if it is too soon for me to go back? I'd humbly appreciate your opinion on this. I have always respected what you have to say.'

The Duchess listened patiently, her lips pursed and her hands crossed on her lap.

'I suspected this might be the case,' she said. Her voice was quieter than usual and markedly less imperious. 'Everyone expects so much of you. They've seen all the big wins and just want more and more. No one cares to remember you have lost a brother, a son, and a wife in the space of a few short years.'

Fred stayed silent. It was such a relief to have articulated what he felt and even more so that the Duchess had not dismissed him on the spot. He hardly dare look at his companion because he felt so emotional speaking out.

'Apart from anything, I wonder if people realise what an exhausting life you lead,' the Duchess continued. 'I don't just mean the constant dieting, although heaven knows how you do that. I certainly couldn't live off your diet. I mean the constant travelling. You are always off to some far-flung corner of England and, as we all know, the railways are pretty unforgiving. I can't bear them myself. Even your beloved horses are not the most comfortable mode of travel. It must all be a tremendous strain.'

'I do enjoy the races,' Fred broke in, interrupting the Duchess in his keenness to show his joy that someone understood his trials. 'I can hear what you say about the hardships and it can be difficult sometimes, but I also always know it is worth it. Well, at least when I am feeling in a good frame of mind. Then there is nothing like the feeling of winning.'

The Duchess smiled.

'Then there is your answer,' she said. 'You need to get into the right frame of mind. It won't be easy, I know, but if you keep doing what you do so well, it will start to feel better. I know everyone says time heals and it really is infuriating to hear it said time after time, but it is right. Mind you, whenever anyone said it to me after both of my dear husbands died, I thought they were mad. I was delighted to be shot of them and couldn't have been happier!'

Fred laughed.

'Ah, that is better. You have a lovely laugh that lights up your whole face. You just need to do it more. Now, you were supposed to be telling me about that race. Is it true what I heard about Mr Cannon...'

The Duchess was in her element. She loved horse racing and fell upon any gossip she learned like a dog with a bone. Half the time, the stories people fed her with were so far from the truth as to be comical, but that didn't seem to bother her. She just loved knowing she had close access to some of the most well-known characters in racing.

Fred was more than happy to oblige now and began to talk animatedly about the race. He felt relaxed now. It had been so good to share his thoughts with someone and the Duchess was such a good listener. He began to hope things would get better and, like the Duchess, he was now sure the answer lay in racing. Racing was the distraction he needed, and better still, it kept him out of Falmouth House, which was a lonely, empty place since Helen had passed.

After that discussion, Fred threw himself into the season with a gusto which surprised even those who knew him well. He racked up a few good big wins in quick succession, much to the crowd's delight, but of course everyone's eyes were on the derby. There were so many exciting contenders that year, excitement was at fever pitch over who would be riding who and which horse would show the best form on the day.

As it turned out, Mat's early analysis of the coveted Epsom race was spot on. Fred Webb was the jockey to ride on Paradox and all anyone could talk about was the big contest between Fred Archer on Melton and Fred Webb on Paradox. Everyone already sensed this contest would be talked about for years to come.

Fred prepared well for the race, but on the derby day itself had to draw on every ounce of strength to keep that focus. The tension in the crowd was palpable and everyone seemed to be jostling to get close to Fred, when all he wanted to do was be left alone to prepare. The jockey longed for all the preparations to be over, so he could get out to the start line and do his job. To keep himself calm, he went over and over his race plan in his head. By the time they were under starter's orders, he had run the race in his head at least twenty times over.

At last they were off. From the very start it proved to be the nail-biting race everyone had hoped and expected it to be. Paradox quickly managed to get clear out in front, as usual, and for a long while looked like he would be a certain winner. That is, until the pack thinned out and his unusual behaviour kicked in. Webb, who was not anywhere near as talented or experienced as Fred, struggled to find a way to encourage his ride to recover its form. Meanwhile, Fred, on Melton, steadily made ground.

Fred never once took his eyes off his quarry. To him it was as though there were no one else in the race. He didn't move up though. He deliberately kept Melton at a distance. Webb must have been aware of his presence, but couldn't quite spot Fred. He tipped his head back as far as he dared, but couldn't quite make him out. His rival had positioned himself perfectly.

Fred skilfully kept Melton back until fifty yards from the post. Then he pounced, urging on his horse, the roars of the crowd ringing in their ears. It was Paradox who sensed Melton first, even before his rider and the horse suddenly put in an unexpected spurt of speed. The race was on. For Fred, with the winning line getting closer and closer, it was now or never. He went for his whip and hit Melton twice with two tremendous strokes using all his strength. It was crude, but effective and Melton shot forward at an explosive pace. The crowd seemed to collectively hold its breath as the two horses thundered side-by-side to the finishing line. In a matter of seconds, they drew level with the post and then it fell behind them. Not a person in the crowd dared make a call on who had won that day.

Everyone craned their necks to watch the horses make their way back to the enclosure. Stewards ran back and forth clutching pieces of paper and consulting in little huddles.

Fred found his space in the winner's enclosure and dismounted. He was just yards away from Webb. They acknowledged each other with a nod, but didn't say a word. They both felt equally strongly about the race. Losing for either man would be devastating. Fred was convinced his rival had a smug look on his face, clearly sure he had won. He self-consciously smoothed down Lord Hasting's colours of eau-de-Nil and crimson. He hoped he had not let his patron down.

There was a commotion in the crowd.

'They've put the numbers up!' someone shouted.

'It's Melton!' said another.

The crowd began to clap and roar its approval, wild in its excitement.

Fred glanced over at Webb. His face was ashen. It

was the fifth year in a row he had come second to Fred Archer in the derby. He was a truly beaten man.

Within moments, a large crowd amassed around Fred. Lord Hastings strode through the middle of the throng and warmly congratulated the jockey.

'Extraordinary race,' he said, pumping Fred's hand up and down. 'Extraordinary. I have never seen such an exciting race. Never seen such talent and sheer grim determination.'

Fred smiled. He knew he had ridden a good race too and was pleased with himself. He had done exactly what he set out to do and his plan had worked to perfection.

The race was later described in the Press as 'Archer's Masterpiece' and confirmed his place as the master tactician. The race also ensured Fred's place as one of the wealthiest jockeys ever known. Lord Hastings's reward to Fred was lavish by any standards: £4,525, which represented half his stake. Archer even received a telegram from a renowned playwright, novelist and poet which read:

'I understand that Milton's 'Paradise Lost' is being revived and will appear in Derby Week and will be published under the title 'Paradox Lost' by Melton.'

Fred was bemused by the adoration of his fan-base. He knew well how fickle the crowd could be, but for now he was rather enjoying being the golden boy once again. Life certainly felt a little more optimistic than it had of late. It was optimistic with an edge, though. While Fred was surrounded by a large base of loyal supporters, many had taken to calling him 'the demon'. There was, it had been widely surmised and agreed upon, an almost demonic power around Fred Archer's riding style. He had to win. Every time. Come what may.

Those that saw him ride were mesmerised by his skill but would also remark upon the fact it seemed to be all he lived for. He seemed to get no pleasure from winning race after race. He would simply turn up at the track, cast his opposition aside in his wake, sail through the winning line, accept his prize and move on.

That season he rode an astonishing 246 winners. It was, by any measure, an incredible achievement and he had proved he was one of the greatest jockeys of all time.

Sadly, this extraordinary success did not bring Fred Archer the happiness he yearned for.

CHAPTER TWELVE

The 1886 racing season did not begin well for Fred. The constant fasting and poor diet was beginning to take a toll on his health. He found it harder and harder each spring to get his weight down to the punishing level it needed to be and he felt like he had less and less reserves of strength to do what needed to be done. Fred had been wasting now for thirteen years and he was beginning to look noticeably unwell. Close friends such as Sam, Joe, and Molly told him this again and again, but he took no notice.

'I know you need to keep the weight down, old chap, but there has to be a better way,' Joe would urge. 'You look really sick.'

Molly tried a different tactic, encouraging the cook to prepare very small, yet extremely tempting portions of Fred's favourite dishes. He'd either push them around the plate, or refuse to even sit at the table, stomping off to take yet another Turkish bath.

To make things even more difficult this year, his mentor, friend, and confidant, Mat Dawson, had retired. Mat's new home, Exning Manor House, was just two miles northeast of Newmarket but it felt like the other side of the world to Fred. Up until then, he hadn't realised how much he still relied on the opinion of the trainer. While Mat had passed on his share of Heath House to his nephew George, this meant little to Fred who barely acknowledged his new business partner. As far as Fred was concerned, Mat was his confidant and sounding board when it came to horses and always had been. Fred got into the routine of travelling out to confer with him most weekends, but he felt like a bond had been broken. Everything seemed very different.

Fred felt deeply frustrated by his present situation. It had barely registered how well organised Mat had been with their retainers in the past, but it did now. To be honest, Fred had always taken Mat Dawson a little for granted. He did what he was good at and left the business side down to the older man, who had always done it so well. All of a sudden, the Heath House stables felt chaotic and disorganised. Fred was never sure who he should be riding and it troubled him. Also, while everyone in the racing community had huge respect for Fred's abilities, it was Mat Dawson that did all the big negotiations and who kept the patrons informed and happy. Fred found juggling the needs of owners and managing a busy stables very difficult indeed.

There were financial pressures too. Despite the successes of the '85 season, his betting had not gone well in recent times. He was speculating more heavily than ever but things had not always gone his way. Meanwhile, his father William was still sending bills his way for settlement, if anything more frequently than ever and in ever greater amounts. As always, Fred didn't think twice about paying them.

Fred's first race of the new season, the Two Thousand Guineas, seemed to confirm the widespread fears he was struggling. He came a poor fourth on Saraband after a lacklustre performance and seemed to be struggling to find his form. Perhaps the shock of the poor start fired him up a little, because he managed to recover enough in time for the derby where he had a convincing win on Ormonde, but it was clear to those closest to him, the races were taking their toll and his riding was becoming erratic. Privately, Fred felt the same. He didn't say as much, but he firmly believed that almost any half decent jockey could have won on Ormonde, since the horse was on such fine form. Perhaps though, this self-criticism was simply another sign of his ailing health and poor state of mind.

As happened so frequently now, he visited the Duchess and spoke freely to her of his doubts.

'You have to do exactly what you did last season,' she urged. 'You took my advice then and look how well it turned out for you.'

Fred was silent. The Duchess noticed that Fred was becoming increasingly withdrawn these days. Some days he would barely say anything at all. It was a testament to her great affection for the young man that she accepted this and merely tried to cajole him into feeling more content. Her other visitors would have been given very short shrift indeed if they had been this inattentive to the noblewoman.

'What about the Ascot Gold Cup?' the Duchess continued. 'Now, that is something to concentrate on. Didn't you say you were rather anxious to win that for the first time? Where were you placed last year?'

'Second,' Fred said quietly.

'Well, there you are,' the Duchess said triumphantly. 'It pays to have something to look forward to. It really does. I often say it and am invariably proved right. Now, what about St Mirin?'

Fred looked up at the Duchess and smiled. They both knew St Mirin was not having a good season either. He was a good colt that had been marked out for greater things, but had never quite managed to attain them. Fred very much doubted he was the jockey to coax the best performance out of St Mirin, particularly on his current showing. The Duchess read his look and correctly judged exactly what he was thinking.

'Oh, come, come, you know he can do better things in the right hands and if anyone has the right hands, you do,' she said.

Fred looked down at his hands, turning them slowly palm upwards and nodded slowly.

'It seems we both have something to prove this season, myself and St Mirin,' he said at last. 'It will be the perfect pairing.'

'Delightful,' the Duchess exclaimed, clapping her hands.

Despite the Duchess' enthusiasm, it was quickly apparent the outside world did not share her optimism. Indeed, not long after this conversation,

Fred ran into the Duke of Beaufort, who told him in no uncertain terms that he was 'absurdly wrong' to be confident in St Mirin.

'I've seen him run and he doesn't have the form,' the Duke told Fred flatly.

If Fred was inwardly infuriated, he didn't show it. He knew by now how to speak to rich patrons and kept his tone light.

'We may yet surprise you,' he smiled. 'The Duchess of Montrose seems pretty convinced and she has a good eye.'

Not long after this conversation, Fred placed a huge bet on St Mirin which was being given very long odds indeed. He also urged all his friends to do the same.

'He's a winner,' he said. 'You'll make a fortune.'

Joe, who now was more worried about his friend than ever, had very real concerns that Fred was throwing his money about more in a bid to appease his own doubts than for any real belief he was riding a potential winner. His behaviour was certainly becoming more and more erratic.

In preparation for Ascot, it was agreed Fred would also ride St Mirin in the Cambridgeshire. The week before this event, Fred travelled to Ireland to ride Cambusmore at the Curragh October Meeting. As usual, his good friend Joe accompanied him and as they crossed on the ferry, Fred had a conversation with Joe that really alarmed him.

'Did you hear about those burglaries?' Fred began. 'There have been more and more around our way. I told the valet to take my revolver and sleep with it by his bed while I am away.'

Joe looked at Fred sharply.

'You can't be serious?' he exclaimed. 'That can't be safe.'

Fred shrugged.

'Better safe than sorry. I've told him to return it to my bedside table when I get back.'

Joe looked incredulous.

'I've told you before, it is hugely unlikely that anyone will break into Falmouth House and, even if they do, you can't just shoot them. You will get into more trouble than the burglar! What would happen if you injured him, or worse still, killed him?'

'It would teach them a lesson, wouldn't it?' Fred said darkly.

He was staring straight ahead, his expression utterly blank. Joe shook his head. Some days he would swear that he hardly recognised his friend. He had changed so much in the past few years.

When they arrived at the course, Fred received some bad news at the weigh in. He tipped the scales at 9 stone 4 pounds, even after shedding his jacket and waistcoat. Somehow he had managed to completely misread the conditions which meant he needed to shed a further 4 pounds to ride Cambusmore at the correct weight. This was no mean feat if he had the luxury of a couple of weeks to do so, certainly not a couple of days. To make things even more challenging, he received a last moment invitation to ride Isidore for another owner, but to achieve the right weight for this race, he needed to be

8 stone 7 pounds.

'Just say it is impossible,' urged Joe. 'You look terrible, Fred. It is not right to even expect to lose more than half a stone in a day. It is inhuman. Can you imagine what damage you are doing to your body?'

'I'm fine,' Fred mumbled. 'Isidore is a dead cert. I have to take this ride. It isn't till the day after tomorrow. That is plenty of time.'

He clearly wasn't fine. He even seemed a little delirious.

That evening, Fred and Joe went to the theatre at the invitation of one of the rich proprietors. They saw *The Mikado*, but Joe wasn't sure his friend really took much of it in. His expression was blank for much of the time. He barely even seemed to register the crowds which followed them back to their hotel shouting his name. He went straight to his room with barely a backwards glance to say goodnight to Joe.

The following day, Fred spent almost the entire day in the Turkish baths, having dosed himself up with a dangerously large quantity of the special mash he had brought along with him. Joe hung around, hoping to spend some time with his friend, but Fred carefully avoided all company.

The next morning, Fred woke early and went straight to the weighing room. This time he tipped the scales at just 8 stone, 12 pounds. It wasn't where he wanted to be, but it meant he had lost an astonishing six pounds in twenty-four hours.

Discovering his friend had already gone, Joe raced down to the weighing room to intercept him before the race. As Fred walked out, Joe gasped in surprise.

Fred Archer looked like a walking skeleton. His face had a dreadful pale grey pallor, and there were large, dark rings below his eyes. His legs looked stick thin beneath his jodhpurs and Joe could have sworn that Fred's hands were shaking a little.

'Morning Fred,' Joe said brightly. He knew better than to kick off by questioning his friend on the day of a race. He already had a look of utter concentration on his face. 'All set?'

'All set,' Fred nodded.

His voice sounded gravelly and didn't seem to have any of its usual authority and surety.

'Your first ride in Ireland,' Joe said, falling into step beside him. 'I can't believe you've not been here before.'

'Better make it count,' Fred said. He was staring at the course ahead of him.

Just then a huge cheer went up from the crowds around the enclosure. Fred may not have ridden there before, but everyone knew him very well. People automatically broke out into applause and Fred smiled and nodded in recognition.

'They seem pretty excited,' Joe said. 'Or maybe it is in appreciation of all the wasting you've done. I don't think I ever saw you look half as bad as you do now.'

Fred laughed and patted his stomach ruefully.

'If I look bad now, just imagine what I will be like next week. I'm riding St Mirin at 8 stone 6 pounds in Cambridgeshire. I've got to go down the same amount again.'

Joe gave a low whistle.

'Freddie, I really think you might want to reconsider. Tell the Duchess it is not possible and you are feeling under the weather. We can find a replacement.'

Fred gave a low laugh.

'Tell the Duchess "no"?' he said. 'Not many people have done that and lived to tell the tale. She is not used to refusals.'

He dug deep into his pocket and pulled out a piece of folded paper.

'I received this at the hotel this morning. It is a telegram from the Duchess. She must have been worried my ardour was waning. Go on, read it.'

Joe unfolded the telegram and read.

'My horse runs in the Cambridgeshire. I count on you to ride it – Montrose.'

'Short and to the point,' Joe said, handing the slip of paper back to Fred.

'Indeed,' nodded Fred. 'So there is no backing out. One barrel of special mash coming up, followed by a week melting in the baths.'

The pair laughed. Joe noted it was nice to see Fred in relatively good spirits, despite his obvious discomfort.

Somehow, despite all that he had been through, the Curragh October Meeting didn't work out too badly either. Fred somehow managed to find the energy to ride two cracking races, winning comfortably on both Cambusmore and Isidore, much to the delight of the crowds.

After returning to Falmouth House, Fred spent almost all of the next week in the Turkish baths, after again dosing himself up with large quantities of special mash, just as he said he would do. In the final three days before the Cambridgeshire, Fred touched no food at all.

Now, for the first time in his life, he felt forced to admit he was beginning to feel weak and ill. On the morning of the race he confided in Molly who, like Joe, was beside herself with worry at how gaunt and sickly Fred was becoming.

'I really think you should reconsider this race,' she said gently. 'You know I have never ever interfered in what you do, but you just don't look yourself. Why don't you take a few weeks off and let me look after you?'

'I've never ridden a winner at Cambridgeshire,' Fred said quietly. 'I have this strange feeling that if I don't succeed this time, I will never get the chance again.'

'Oh, what nonsense,' Molly tutted. 'You're not doing yourself any favours. There will be other years. Of course there will be. You are one of the most successful jockeys that ever lived. Let the Duchess boss someone else around for a week or two. I'm happy to tell her that, mind. Don't you worry.'

Fred laughed softly, despite how badly he felt. He knew how passionately Molly cared for him and wouldn't put it past her to give the Duchess a piece of her mind. He wasn't quite sure who would win in that battle of wills either, but didn't particularly want to be there to find out.

'No, don't do that,' he said hurriedly. 'I'm doing this for me, more than anything else. St Mirin is a great colt and you know how much I like to prove everyone wrong.'

'But you are not yourself,' Molly said, unable to hide her exasperation. 'Let me look after you.'

'I'm fine, I'm fine.'

Fred would not hear of pulling out of the race and was still convinced he was right about St Mirin too. This was in the face of a very clear message from the bookies that they disagreed with this opinion: St Mirin was given odds of 100-8.

As Fred travelled to the track he went over and over the race in his mind. It frustrated him how difficult he found it to do this these days. In the past it had come so naturally. These days he'd all too easily lose track of where he was and need to begin again. If he was interrupted by a wellwisher, as he often was, he would lose focus entirely and have an internal battle with himself to get back to where he had been. In some cases he found it easier to ignore the cheery greetings of others at the track, which was beginning to cause enormous offense among those who knew Fred well.

By the time he reached starters orders, Fred was feeling more lightheaded and giddy than ever. The excitement and adrenalin of the forthcoming race had driven his food deprived system into overdrive. His heart beat faster than he had ever experienced before and the blood pulsed hard at his temples. Sweat dropped off his brow, even though the day was cool and there was a stiff breeze blowing.

The race began badly for Fred. Two horses, Carlton and Melton, surged out in front, goading each other on and leaving St Mirin trailing in their wake. Fred used his whip mercilessly but couldn't seem to gain ground. It was only when Melton inexplicably raised his head and dropped back his pace, that Fred was able to find the form he was so convinced lay inside St Mirin. He urged his ride on and managed to find a place clear out in front. Even then, he was far too much of an experienced jockey to let himself relax and he continued to urge St Mirin forward. It was just as well too. In the closing stages of the race, Sailor Prince, a complete outsider, came out of nowhere and crossed the line at the same time as St Mirin.

As Fred rode back to the enclosure, he gripped St Mirin tightly with his knees. He felt so dizzy now, it was all he could do to keep himself upright. If he moved just a few inches to the right or left, he was convinced he would have fallen off altogether.

'Fred, Fred, over here.'

Fred was relieved to hear the familiar voice of Joe, who leapt forward and grabbed St Mirin's reins.

'I think I got it,' Fred gulped. 'No, no, maybe I didn't. I, I just don't know.'

Joe frowned. His friend sounded more disorientated and distant than ever.

'Down you get,' he said, helping Fred from the horse.

Fred landed on the grass with a thud and was very unsteady on his feet. He had to lean forward against the horse's flank to steady himself. Joe began sorting out the saddle, a job Fred had always done as a matter of course. It was clear the jockey just didn't have the strength.

A huge cheer went up in the crowd. Fred didn't even look up. Joe put a hand on his shoulder.

'I'm sorry,' he said.

Fred shook his head as he slowly drew himself up to an upright position. Joe noticed he was so pale now, so as to be almost translucent.

'I've let everyone down...' Fred mumbled.

'...No, no, you ran a great race,' interrupted Joe.

'But I lost. I lost the race. I lost a huge bet. I've lost the Duchess her stake and yet again I have failed to win at Cambridgeshire. It was completely my fault. I don't know what I was thinking. Those two went out so hard, I let them kid me. I changed my strategy mid-race. I'd never normally do that. What was I thinking about, chasing after them like that? I didn't have anything left to take on Sailor Prince. I rode like a bloody amateur.'

Fred was panting now after his outburst. The effort of speaking was almost too much and he leaned into St Mirin again. The horse shifted its weight uncomfortably and snorted in protest.

'Come on old chap. You really don't look well. Let's just get you weighed and get you back to Falmouth house. You need some rest.'

Fred allowed Joe to lead him around, directing him through the usual post-race routine, step by step. He felt like a broken man and was relieved when he finally got home and crawled into bed. Molly fixed him a cup of boiling water and took his temperature.

'You see, you do have a fever,' she said, only a little triumphantly. 'I told you you shouldn't race. I shall fetch the doctor.'

'No, no doctor,' Fred growled. 'I just need to rest.'

Molly tutted and left the room. She decided then and there to write to Emma. Fred's mother would know what to do. This had gone on long enough. The man was clearly unwell.

A letter was duly despatched and in the meantime Molly did everything she could to ensure Fred rested. Fred, for his part, resisted all attempts to keep him in bed and insisted on fulfilling his usual duties in the yard. He was still, Molly noted, barely eating a morsel.

'I've got a race on Wednesday,' he said irritably, when Molly offered him a light meal.

'But it is just a soup,' she insisted bravely. 'It's your favourite too.'

'No soup.'

A letter arrived from Emma the morning Fred set off for Brighton. She said she was on her way with Emily and would be there as soon as she had arranged some affairs at the hotel. In the meantime, she urged Molly to dissuade Fred from racing. It was, however, too late. Fred was already at the racetrack.

To be fair, he very quickly regretted his decision. The wind that blew down the exposed Brighton Downs was bitterly cold and played havoc with his fever. One minute he felt boiling hot and the next moment he felt like he had been plunged into an ice bath. Poor Fred couldn't seem to take control of his body and his limbs were not cooperating at all. This was very much reflected in his terrible performance on the track and he lost three races in a row, each on very well fancied horses. After being beaten out of a place while riding Tommy Tittlemouse, Fred threw in the towel.

'Joe, Joe, please will you help see me home,' he said, grasping his friend's arm. 'I really don't feel very well now.'

Joe's face creased into a picture of concern.

'Of course, of course,' he said quietly. 'You should never have come here in the first place.'

He helped Fred onto a carriage and asked the driver to take them to the train station. Once there, he helped Fred into a private carriage.

'Just wait there a moment,' he said and ducked off outside.

Joe returned a few moments later, carefully carrying a cup. Fred was slumped in the corner of his chair, his eyes closed and his breathing laboured.

'Try this,' he said.

'What is it?' Fred groaned.

'Arrow root and brandy. My old mother swore by it. Cures everything from gout to flu and a bit in between.'

Fred gave a weak smile and took a sip.

'Not sure I want to make a habit of drinking this,' he grimaced. 'It is disgusting.'

'Well, start looking after yourself and get better and you won't have to,' Joe said, indicating with a gesture that Fred should finish the whole cup. 'You need to look after yourself, you know. You really do. You have to start seeing that you have everything to live for: a beautiful daughter, an adoring public who lap up your every move, a family that adore you and a good few bob in your pocket.'

Fred gave a hollow laugh.

'Yes, that is true, I have a lot to be grateful for,' he said. Then he added quietly: 'I would give it all away for just one more smile from her sweet lips.'

With a whistle and a groan, the train slowly steamed out of the station to begin its journey north. Within a few moments Fred was fast asleep and he slept most of the way back to Newmarket while Joe anxiously watched over him.

'How are you feeling now, old chum?' Joe said, as he shook him awake when they arrived at their destination.

Fred blinked in the bright daylight.

'Much better actually. Remind me to write to your mother to congratulate her on her secret brew. I shall be back on racing form in days, that is for sure.'

Joe patted his shoulder and smiled.

'You are still going back to Falmouth House to rest,' he said. 'I'm handing you over to Molly now, so you won't be able to argue.'

Fred made a faint gesture of resignation and got into the waiting carriage. It took him straight to Falmouth House and, as predicted, he was ushered straight into his bed.

'Your mother is here tomorrow,' Molly said, bustling around, closing the curtains and plumping his pillows. 'Believe me, she will want to see you better. Your sister Emily is coming too. With both of them here, you'll have to listen to sense.'

Fred closed his eyes and drifted off back to sleep. It was good to be home.

By the following morning, Fred's illness had taken a distinct turn for the worse. His temperature was far too high and he seemed unable to speak clearly or coherently. Molly sent for a doctor who spent some time in the jockey's room and then sent for another doctor to confirm his initial diagnosis. The two medical men concurred that Fred Archer was suffering from a severe bout of typhoid fever.

'Is it serious?' Molly asked the first doctor, Dr Wright, when they met in the corridor outside Fred's room. She spoke in a hushed tone, tears pricking the corner of her eyes.

'It can be, but he was quite lucid a few moments ago,' Dr Wright replied. He sounded reassuringly matter-of-fact. 'I've seen worse cases, certainly. We need to keep his fluids up, so plenty of water. If you could get some soup down him, that might really help. He looks very undernourished.' Molly gulped hard. She was finding it all too much to bear.

'You need to find a way to keep his spirits up, so he can fight it himself,' went on the doctor. 'He seems very downhearted. I've been attending Fred Archer for fourteen years now and he really does seem to be in a terrible depression of late. Of course, it is all perfectly understandable, but we all need to rally around for him.'

'I'll do my best, sir. His mother, Mrs Archer, will

be here soon. She always knows the right thing to say to him. His sister too.'

'Ah, excellent. I will leave him in your capable hands then. I need to make a few calls this morning, but I will return around noon to check on him.'

The doctor tipped his hat and headed off towards the staircase.

'I'll show myself out,' he called over his shoulder.

Molly sighed and headed back into Fred's room. He seemed to be asleep, so she straightened his covers and settled down into a chair beside the bed. She wanted to be there in case he awoke and needed something.

Mid-morning, Molly heard the door opening downstairs and rushed down to greet her visitors. She found Emily in the hallway, looking anxious as she took off her coat and hat.

'How is he?' she said, forgetting to even greet Molly in her anxiousness to hear about her brother.

'Much the same I am afraid,' Molly said, stepping forward to help the young woman with her coat. 'Where is your mother?'

'She's right behind me,' Emily said, making her way to the staircase. 'She stopped to collect a tonic from Mrs Dawson. The two of them have been corresponding and Mrs Dawson is convinced this is what he needs to build up his strength.'

'The doctor said he will be here at midday,' Molly called to her retreating figure.

By now Emily was halfway up the stairs, taking them two at a time in a bid to see her brother. She paused outside his room and then quietly entered. The room was dimly lit, but she was shocked to see how gaunt and pale Fred looked. It didn't seem possible that this was her handsome, athletic brother. What could possibly have happened?

Emily walked softly across the floor and settled into a chair. She gently picked up Fred's hand, which was cold and slightly clammy. Fred was quiet, but a little restless, tossing and turning in his bed as though he was having nightmares. A few times he cried out and moaned. Once he shouted Helen's name. Emily watched him tirelessly.

As the clock ticked closer to noon, Emily got up to stretch her legs. The doctor would be back soon and she was feeling stiff and uncomfortable after her long journey, followed by a short spell in the chair. She wandered over to the window and pulled the thick curtain to one side to peer down at the garden below. The grass didn't look its best and had a thick covering of brown and orange oak leaves.

'Are they coming?'

The voice startled her so much that she let out an involuntary gasp. It was Fred, clearly, yet didn't sound like Fred at all. Emily immediately swung around and almost screamed in shock. Fred was half in, half out of the bed, clutching a revolver in his hand. His expression was blank. It was almost as if he were still asleep.

Without thinking, Emily rushed forward, grabbing Fred's right wrist, the one which had the revolver in the hand, and gave it a sharp jolt. She didn't really have a plan. Instinct just took over. She just knew she had to do everything she could to make him drop the weapon.

Using his other hand, Fred pushed her roughly away. Emily was overwhelmed by how strong Fred was. He twisted his wrist and managed to shake her off as though she was a child clutching at its mummy's skirts.

Suddenly, Emily felt Fred's right arm curled, snake-like around her neck and she experienced a tremendous force downwards as he used her to support himself as he got unsteadily to his feet. Emily's two hands shot up into the air and began to madly paw at Fred's arm, desperately trying to free herself from his vicelike grip. In the struggle, Fred staggered back two paces, dragging Emily with him her legs dangling helplessly like a rag doll, before they both slammed up against the door, their joint weight pushing it tightly shut.

The room, which had been so quiet, was now filled with the sound of screams. Emily realised it was her that was screaming in a rapid burst of desperate shrieks. She sounded like a wounded animal battling for its last breath. She felt Fred's weight shift, then the faintest of clicks and in an instant she heard the loudest noise she had ever heard in her life. Propelled forward by she didn't know what, she fell to the ground in a heap with the lifeless form of Fred slumped across her legs.

'No, no, no,' she screamed. 'Fred! Fred!'

Twisting and turning to free herself from the weight pinning down her legs, she screamed with all her might. Her shrieks became louder and more hysterical with each breath. When she could scream no more, Emily was quiet. Tears fell down her cheeks as she stared at the river of blood that was flowing from a hole in the side of Fred's cheek. She turned her gaze away and her eyes fell upon the small, grey revolver, lying abandoned on the floor.

In the distance she became vaguely aware of the sound of running and shouting. The sounds got closer and closer to the door. Emily sat up, her back leaning against the bed, her knees drawn to her chest, eyes staring madly at the sight she could hardly bear to see. She was shaking now and felt hot, dizzy, and sick.

The first person who burst through the door was Emma. Her scream echoed around the house and seemed to last for an eternity.

AFTERWORD

'There you are. I have been searching everywhere for you. All the guests are leaving now. William has asked me to take Scotch Pearl home with me. I told him that after all the rides Freddie and I shared together, it would be an honour.'

Emma was standing at the window looking down at the sombre two lines of carriages slowly snaking their way up and down Falmouth House's drive. Down below her, a number of people dressed almost entirely in black milled around the grand stone steps that marked the entrance to the house.

'That is nice,' she said quietly. 'Thank you Edward. I just needed a few moments alone. I know it is strange, considering what happened in here, but I find it a comfort to be in Fred's room. I'm standing in the last place where he ever was.'

Lord James walked forward and placed his hands gently on Emma's shoulders. With no trace of self-consciousness he bent down and lightly kissed the top of her head.

'I know I cannot even begin to imagine what you are going through,' he began. 'The shock of losing dear Freddie is almost inconceivable and to see it too.'

He stopped speaking as he saw large tears beginning to fall down Emma's cheeks.

'He was only twenty-nine years of age,' Emma sobbed. 'A parent should not live to bury two of her children.'

Lord James was silent. There really were no words.

'What sort of life did he have?' Emma gulped. 'Whisked away from his family when he was a child, forced to live in stable quarters with dozens of boys, being bullied and working his fingers to the bone. He was always such a sensitive boy.'

'But he lived an incredible life,' Lord James interjected. 'He grew up to become the best known jockey on the track. The crowds adored him and cheered him everywhere he went. Everyone wanted to be close to him. Owners used to fight over whose horses he would ride.'

'But they were fickle too, weren't they?' Emma shot back. 'We all saw how it could change on a whim. One moment he was the top of the pile and the next moment he was being accused of throwing races. Everyone was hostile and whispering things behind his back. Even the newspapers were writing nasty things.'

'It happens,' Lord James said, with a resigned shrug. 'The racetrack is a tense place. Fortunes are won and lost in a few moments. People are bound to get carried away. They always came back to Fred though, didn't they? They adored him. You only had to be at the funeral today to see that. The whole of Newmarket came to a standstill. I've never seen so many flowers. Everyone could see what a remarkable talent he had.'

'But it was a hard won talent, wasn't it? How many people realised what he went through to get it? All the fasting and wasting. Poor child. Some weeks he would barely eat a thing. No wonder he became so ill. He was trying to lose more than one stone in weight in the week he died.'

'It wasn't just the wasting though, or the racing, was it?' Lord James broke in. 'Losing Helen was a tremendous blow for him. When I saw him at her funeral, I wondered then how he would ever recover and I don't think he ever did.'

Emma stared out the window. Below her, the Duchess of Montrose was being helped into her carriage by a footman in smart livery. The woman looked entirely changed. Normally she stood proud, straight-backed and imperious. Today she was hunched in grief and was dabbing at her cheeks with a handkerchief. Emma watched as Lord Falmouth stopped at her carriage and leaned in to say a few words.

'They are all here,' Emma said, her voice cracking with emotions. 'Lords, ladies, owners and stable lads. Well, except my husband William, who can't even bear to leave the house now. Everyone wants to be close to Fred, even in death. But where were they? Why did no one see how ill he had become? Why was there no one to protect him?'

Lord James squeezed Emma's shoulders once

more and his hands dropped limply to his side. He walked across the room, shaking his head as though trying to force the right words from his brain.

'They tried, they really did,' he said. 'You saw how broken Joe was at the service today. He could barely get through the reading he was so choked up. I spoke with him afterwards. He said he repeatedly warned Fred to ease off, but he just wouldn't.

'You know what he was like, Emma. We all knew and loved that look he used to get in his eyes when he thought about winning. It was what kept him going. In a way, it was all that kept him going after he lost Helen.'

Emma stayed silent. Lord James searched within himself for something else to stop the agony tearing apart the woman he loved so deeply.

'I spoke to Molly,' he said, his voice faltering at the memory. 'She was the last one at the graveside, along with Bert. They waited behind to leave the sweetest posy of dried flowers. She said it was the same ones that Fred had put on their pony and trap to take her to church to marry Bert. She'd kept them all these years because they were so special. They wanted Fred to have them because *he* was so special. And he was. You have to know that.'

The room lapsed into silence and Emma continued to watch the scene below. She shuddered as she saw her dear friend Mary Rose leading Grace off in the direction of the Dawsons' carriage. *That poor family*, she thought. *They've had more than their share of tragedy too.*

'What now?' she whispered. 'What now?'

Lord James strode back across the room and picked up her hand. Looking earnestly into her eyes he pleaded with her with his own.

'Now we make the most of our lives. If there is one thing this has shown us, it is that life is cruelly short. We should all grasp what happiness we can, when we can.'

Emma pulled her hand back and turned away.

'How can you even say this?' she moaned. 'You know I feel this is somehow my fault? This is my punishment for, for... what happened. No, no, we cannot blindly follow our hearts. Love only leads to heartache and disappointment.'

'That's not true!' Lord James cried. 'Fred was happy. He had the best years of his life with Helen. They loved each other more in a short space of time than some people get to feel for each other in a lifetime. It was intense and cruelly stopped short, but I know Fred would never have swapped the opportunity of at least some time with the love of his life, for anything else.

'Your Freddie was a remarkable man, who rose to become a world figure in racing and who even managed to overcome his tremendous grief to have a remarkable last season. Celebrate that, be proud of that and be happy for the good times. He enjoyed what he did so much. You know that.'

Emma nodded slowly, reached out and squeezed Lord James' hand between her own. Just then, a squeal of delight and laughter drifted up from the yard below and burst into Freddie's bedroom. The pair looked down to see young Nellie on her beloved

Moss Two that her father had purchased when she was born. Her grandpa William was holding the reins, while Doug held tightly onto his little charge.

Emma couldn't quite make out what they were saying, but could tell by the by-now familiar body language that her husband was telling Nellie to push her heels down. The toddler was ignoring him completely and simply squealing with delight.

'We must go,' Emma smiled softly. 'We'll be missed.'

'Just give me one small sign there is hope for us one day,' Lord James urged as Emma began to walk towards the door.

Emma turned to face him and smiled once again.

'There is always hope,' she said. 'As Fred proved, if one has the courage and the utter, unbending will to win, the world will fall at your feet. Life goes on.'

She let herself out of the room, closing the door softly behind her and headed off purposefully to join Nellie in the yard.

ABOUT THE AUTHOR

Diana Reynolds is the great granddaughter of the racing legend Fred Archer, and has long been inspired to write a love story behind the sportsman, whose life was tragically cut short when he was at the peak of his career.

Diana was born in Norfolk in 1953 and has spent most of her life there, apart from a short spell in Australia where her eldest son Ollie lives with his family. She has two other children, Natasha and Ali, and a stepdaughter Victoria.

Anything to do with horses is, inevitably, in her blood and having ridden since the age of five, first on a donkey then graduating to a pony and a retired hunter, she still loves to ride whenever possible.

Diana is currently writing the sequel to *Just One More Smile*, the story of Nellie Rose, Fred and Helen's only child.

Printed in Great Britain
by Amazon